THIS IS THE WILDEST, FUNNIEST, EARTHIEST BOOK THAT CHICAGO PAPERBACK HOUSE HAS EVER PUBLISHED. HARDCOVER PUBLISHERS WOULD MAKE A BEST-SELLER OUT OF IT—FIVE DOLLARS AND NINETY-FIVE CENTS A COPY. BUT THIS IS A HARDCOVER PAPERBACK ORIGINAL, AND **YOU** CAN MAKE 'POSTMARK OF AMERICA' A BEST-SELLER—FOR ONLY SIXTY CENTS!
CHICAGO PAPERBACK HOUSE

To—
Dorothy Lael Weronko

POSTMARK OF AMERICA

by

TRAVIERS GLENN

All names, people, places, and events are fictional, except the towns, the postmarks of which, are mentioned in POSTMARK OF AMERICA, are all listed in the 1961 edition of the U.S. Official Postal Guide.

WILDSIDE PRESS

POSTMARK OF AMERICA

Copyright © 1962 by Traviers Glenn

1 It was around four oclock in the morning, and my wife Rembrandt was downstairs in the kitchen getting breakfast and fixing my lunch when the telephone rang.

Between guys wanting to hunt or fish with me on my off-duty weeks, and the uncertainties of the little bug-mashing passenger train on which I work, it was not unusual for our phone to ring at such an early hour. I am a postal transportation clerk, assigned to the Windfall (Illinois) & Saganois (same state) R.P.O. (Railway Post Office) and have been for more than forty years—except for the World Wars, when I took time off to help make Democracy safe twice. I make a round trip every day, every other week, between Windfall and Saganois, right down through the middle of my old country of Spunky Ridge.

The reason I was up at four in the morning was because it was my week on the road. Otherwise I wouldn't have been out of bed, chances are. For I am a firm believer that after sixty a person should sleep in unless he wants to hunt or fish.

"Answer the phone, dear," Rembrandt yelled. "Maybe The Folly has been annulled and we can go back to bed."

I was upstairs. I had already shaved, and was in my den fooling with my collection of postmarks. Some new ones had arrived in the mail the day before and I was arranging them in their album so they would form sentences, as all collectors of postmarks do. Four of them, I remember, were "Assawoman, Va," "De Queen, Ark," "Fosters, Ala," and "Intercourse, Pa."

I spend a lot of time with my postmarks, and have a lot of fun with them. As a psychological test they work a good deal like Mr. Rorschach's ink blots. I can give a person a handful of my postmarks and analyze his personality by just studying the way he arranges them. I had used the test on our two daughters-in-law and the marriages were going along fine; and I intended to use it on whomever daughter Shawn decided to marry.

"Answer it yourself," I hollered down the stairway. "I'm like the trouble shooter for the Chicago firm who was in Portland, Oregon when he got a wire from his boss to slip down to El Paso and shoot a piece of trouble. He wired back, 'Slip down yourself, you're 250 miles closer than I am.'"

"I'm frying the eggs."

The phone was still ringing frantically, and when I picked it up and said hello the operator's voice came in clearly, "Is this Mr. Bolander Paydoley, Rural Route No. 1, Windfall, Illinois?"

"Yes, ma'am, it is."

"This is Pistol River, Oregon calling. Your party is ready, Mr. Stambo," the operator said. "Go ahead."

I knew about where Pistol River, Oregon was located: Down in the southwest corner of the state, near the coast. Being a mail-car man for so many years, I naturally would. I even had a Pistol River postmark. I wondered who in the world was calling me from that neck of the woods at four oclock in the morning.

"Mr. Paydoley, this is Attorney John Stambo, of Pistol River, Oregon. Your aunt, Mrs. Prudence Persnosky, was found dead here yesterday."

"Is that so? So she died in the United States, after all. Everybody thought sure she'd die over in India or Australia or someplace like that."

"I have been appointed by the court here to take care of her legal affairs temporarily, and in examining part of her effects I've come to the conclusion that you and a Mrs. Bonnie Dooks Stabbs, of Chicago, are the relatives she considered the most trustworthy. You're her nephew, aren't you?"

"Yes, and Mrs. Stabbs is her niece. Our mothers are her sisters."

"She was a widow, wasn't she?"

"That's right. Her husband died years ago. Couldn't keep up with her."

"She had no children?"

"None." My Uncle Phineas Persnosky shot sailers only, but I didn't know Mr. Stambo well enough yet to tell him that. "What was she doing when she died?"

By this time Rembrandt was hanging over my shoulder, and Shawn in her silkaline pajamas had come down from upstairs.

"She was up here in the mountains in a tourist cabin by herself. Told Mr. Tczetl, the proprietor of the motel, she was going to hunt uranium."

"Told who?"

"Harry Tootle. T-c-z-e-t-l. It's pronounced Tootle."

"Wait till I write that down. Somebody here might want to get in touch with him."

"His address is Skytop Tourist Camp, Pistol River, Oregon."

Hunting uranium sounded exactly like something Aunt Prue would do. She was always looking for ways to help the government. Highly patriotic, she always wrote "Gladly" in front of "Pay to" on the check she sent in with her income-tax report.

"Her car had been parked two days in front of her cabin, and when Harry Tootle went to investigate he looked through the window and saw Mrs. Persnosky stretched out on the davenport. Her eyes were closed, and so was her mouth, and her Geiger counter was beside her. He called to her, and when she didn't answer or move he unlocked the door and went over to her and she was dead."

You can tell a good deal about a man by talking to

him on the phone long distance, and this guy sounded all right. "What has been done, so far?" I asked.

"Well, the first thing Harry did was call our undertaker, Mr. Wang. Charley Wang. He's Chinese."

"I'll write that down too."

"I guess you think we have some odd-sounding names out here."

"No more than anywhere else in the country. My closest neighbor's name is Rump. His wife's name is Fanny." I thought of springing one of Aunt Prue's favorite stories on him, about a man named Joe Stink who went to court to get his name changed, and told the judge "I'm tired of hearing 'Hullo, Joe, whaddye know, I want my name changed to Fred Stink." Aunt Prue had first heard it in the nineteenth century, and never told it unless her audience was of a generation young enough to possibly never heard it. However, I didn't know how old Mr. Stambo was, and besides he was paying for the call and might not appreciate wasting time on such a joke.

"Mr. Wang examined her pocketbook and—"

"Was it that big leather saddlebag she always carried? About two feet each way?"

"That's it. Wang found twenty-three hundred dollars and sixty-nine cents in cash, two thousand dollars in traveler's checks, a bank book, and a sealed envelope marked 'Last Will and Testament of Mrs. Prudence Persnosky' in it."

"Gee whiz!"

"As County Attorney, I was appointed by the County judge to handle the legal matters in the case, and I have taken care of everything."

"What did you do with the money?"

"Put it in the bank here. I loaded everything else in Mrs. Persnosky's car and drove it around to the sheriff's office, locked it and gave the keys to the sheriff.

Contents of the car are just as she left them."

"What kind of car?"

"New Fleetwood Cadillac. Only about 9000 miles on it."

"Cadillac, huh. Gee whiz!"

"By the way, do you know how old she was?"

"Not exactly, but somewhere between eighty and ninety. She was born in the Spunky Ridge section of Illinois, and everybody from down in that country live to be eighty or ninety. I can find out and let you know."

"I wish you would. And I assume you want the body shipped back to Illinois."

"I suppose so. Her husband is buried here."

"Where should the body be sent?"

"Either Windfall or Saganois, whichever is more convenient. Jones' Mortuary at Windfall, or Parker's Funeral Home at Saganois."

I could hear Mr. Stambo repeat the addresses as he wrote them down, and when he was done I asked, "Will somebody have to go out there and bring her back? I wouldn't mind the trip."

"No, I checked on that. Nobody will have to accompany the body, but she will need two tickets."

As an old railroader I knew that. I said, "I guess she'll make it by herself, all right. She always has." That was an odd thing about Aunt Prue: You thought of her as being just as capable and efficient when she was dead as she was when she was alive. "How about her real estate?" I asked. "She had some houses down in Florida, that I know of."

"Her will is sealed and can't be opened until the court gives permission. Also among her effects — all of which the court hasn't had time to examine yet — there may be information concerning all her business details. Remember, she just died yesterday or early this morning — we think — and we haven't had time to do more than what was absolutely necessary. By the way, what time is it there? Around four in the morning?"

"Four-fifteen."

"I know I worked at the office till midnight. I would have called sooner but couldn't find time. Mr. Wang and I selected a nice, medium-priced coffin; and Mrs. Persnosky is dressed in white. I think we've done all we can do for the present."

"We'll go ahead and arrange for the funeral at this end, and you and Mr. Wang can get the body on the road as soon as you can."

"Wang said it would leave today."

"We'll be looking for her. I'm glad you dressed her in white, account of she liked white."

"O.K. I guess that's all then. If necessary, I'll call you or you can call me. And thank you for your courtesy. Goodby."

One thing I knew about Attorney John Stambo for sure, and that was he had been in some branch of military service. That "thank you for your courtesy" was a dead giveaway. I guessed Mr. Stambo went in as a buck private and came out about a buck colonel. Probably he had been in the Air Corps.

I hung up the receiver and said to Rembrandt, "Gee whiz, Aunt Prue's dead."

"The first time I ever saw her she worked for a circus," Brandy said thoughtfully. "Swung by her teeth."

I nodded reflectively, as a person does when, growing older, he realizes he averages going to more and more funerals every year. It's not only a sign he's getting older all the time, but that he has lived a long time in the same place and has made many friends and acquaintances. "Rode horses and elephants, too," I said. "Aunt Prue could do anything. Once she even played the part of a zombie in a movie. She got more fun out of living than anybody I ever knew."

"I always liked her, what little I ever saw of her. She was a lot like you."

I looked at Shawn. Even at four A.M. Shawn was beautiful. She had her mother's dark, wide-apart eyes and long black curly hair, and she had Rembrandt's sweet curve of bosom and length of limb. Shawn was my wife's daughter in appearance, but in no other characteristic.

For something unusual had happened when Shawn was conceived. The Irish Dinnegan blood of my mother should have filtered through me and combined with Rembrandt Foster's gentle genes to produce a typical hybrid American girl. Instead, it had collided with the blood of my half-savage Turkish ancestors, which was flecked here and there with Mesquakie Indian, so that the resultant mixture that charged through Shawn's veins was more like benzine than blood. At twenty-two Shawn had many male scalps dangling from her cummerbund, but none of the scalpings had made her cry.

I felt a little sorry for the man Shawn would some day marry because he would be hooked for a lot of life. It was Shawn instead of me who was a lot like Aunt Prue. Rembrandt, however, could never believe it.

I sat down to breakfast, and protested to Rembrandt, "I don't have quite so much Dinnegan blood in me as she did. Old Grandpa Dinnegan could pick up a barrel of whisky and hold it while he drank out of the bunghole."

"Well, can't you do the same thing, only on a smaller scale — with a keg, for instance?" Rembrandt said.

I have difficulty mustering dignity, but occasionally I try to present some. "The Paydoley blood is not so explosive as the Dinnegan blood," I said stiffly. "It's more civilized and more philosophic. And I was born a generation later. I'd never dream of doing a lot of things Aunt Prue did."

"Four sandwiches enough?"

"How many peanut butter?"

"Two. And there's apple pie."

"Four's enough if two are peanut butter." I'll bet that in the forty years I've been hashing up and down the Windfall & Saganois in a mail car I've eaten a barrel of peanut butter. I began eating peanut butter away back when it could be bought only in bulk. And now that it is put up in attractive jars and is crunchier and creamier I think it is tastier than ever, especially when mixed with honey—first tried out in the navy, I believe. My six grandchildren—with two more in sight —all like it, too. About the first understandable sound they all made was "pee-buh."

"Aunt Prue would have made a good postal transportation clerk," Rembrandt said. "She liked to study maps."

Every person has a list of words and phrases that grate on his ears, and "postal transportation clerk" heads my list—and for no good reason. When the first postmaster general, Lightning Ben Franklin, realized that without some system of communication even the thirteen colonies could not be held together, let alone California and Idaho, and inaugurated wagon postal service between New York and a few towns up and down the east coast, the service had been called simply Postal Service. Then as rail transportation, with distribution of mail enroute, developed and rode roughshod over stage coaches, steamboats and the short-lived Pony Express, the service was called Railway Mail and its employes railway postal clerks.

In the golden age of railroad expansion there was an aura of romance and glamor and prestige surrounding mail-car men. The first ones (before the advent of the Civil Service Commission) were appointed to their jobs by the President; the initials R.P.C. were officially tacked to their names; and they comprised a haughty and efficient group of men who worked without supervision on rail lines all over the country. By 1949, however, there was so much mail being carried by airplanes that the fly people demanded recognition of the fly paper, so all nomenclature was changed. The head man of a mail car, formerly called Clerk-In-Charge, a dignified, lordly and explanatory title, was changed to Foreman. And to an old-timer like me the designation had the same pride-killing connotation as Straw Boss.

I finished breakfast and lit a cigarette. This was the golden hour of plan-making, mind-meeting and heart-to-heart talking, when the stomach is full and the day's activities about to begin. More people should get up a few minutes earlier in order to enjoy it.

Shawn lit her cigarette off mine. "What was she doing away out there in Oregon, anyway? At her age? All by herself?"

"Oh, I don't know. This lawyer Stambo said she was hunting uranium. But maybe she just happened to look at a map of that country and took a notion to go out there. She was always doing that — maps fascinated her."

"I agree with Mom that she would have made a good high-behind." Ever since she was a little girl Shawn had called mail-car men highbehinds. She said they were always reaching down to load mail from a truck into a mail car, or unloading mail from the car to a truck, and thus their behinds were always high. Shows how observant she is.

"She would have made a good anything, even a farmer, which requires more different kinds of knowledge than any job I know of. She and Uncle Phineas lived on a farm awhile, too, but Uncle Phin couldn't stand the hard work. I used to visit them when I was a kid. They had a farm over on Limberswitch, which is the first hogback east of Spunky Ridge, down in Starbuck County.

"I remember one Thanksgiving school vacation when I was about ten I was visiting them and they had a lot of chickens. Uncle Phin was sick in bed, and one chilly, misty night just as we were getting ready to go to bed we heard a big commotion out in the hen house.

"Some varmint had been stealing Aunt Prue's chickens for quite a while, and only the week before she had bought a watch dog. I even remember the dog's name: Obis First Syllable of Astoria. I had read about Joan of Arc, Duke of Cumberland and St. Francis of Assisi, and when Aunt Prue told me Obis' full name I thought he was quite an important dog. It was not till I was in high school studying Latin that I learned the full significance of the title Aunt Prue had bestowed on the dog. She called him Obie for short.

"Down in my old home country of Spunky Ridge night air is supposed to poison sick people, so of course Uncle Phin couldn't get out in it. So Aunt Prue and I went. She got her old double-barrelled shotgun from behind the kitchen door and pushed a couple of shells in it. It was an L.C. Smith. I remember it well. Its two hammers had been lost or broken and somebody had put on another one and it didn't match in looks but worked all right. Funny how a person will remember unimportant things like that and forget important things."

"You know, Boley," Shawn said, "that's the first time I've heard you tell that story since you gave me your first talk on sex: When you explained why Jim Carroll threw me down on a shock of corn and tried to take my panties off."

"Even if you have a good memory, I'm going to finish. It'll help us get into the habit of thinking what kind of person Aunt Prue was, which we'll all have to do during the next few days."

"Good old Greataunt Prue. She was visiting us the first time I menstruated. She told me I had laid my first eggs, and that they were so disappointed at not becoming fertilized that they just got tired waiting and passed out."

"Aunt Prue loaded the old Smith with Nublack shells. Nublack shells — used to buy them for forty-five cents a box of twenty-five, and now shells cost fifteen or twenty cents apiece. They were loaded with black powder, a new explosive that had just been developed — that's where they got their name. Shoot at a rabbit and they boomed out a smoke screen so big and thick you had to duck quick to see whether you had hit it or not.

"We started out to the chicken house, Aunt Prue ahead with the shotgun — both hammers cocked — and me following with the coal-oil lantern with the bull's-eye reflector in its globe.

"In chilly weather Aunt Prue wore men's long-handled underwear, and this night she was in too big a hurry to put on anything else except a pair of overshoes. The newstyle underwear with the flap in the seat had just been invented, and Aunt Prue, always the first to try anything new, was wearing a suit of them. Like everyone else, she never bothered to button the flap.

"Following her with the lantern, I had verified some of my first suspicions of sex. As she walked in a slinking crouch, her shotgun at the ready, the legs on the underwear crinkled first one way and then the other. And by careful timing I could shine the bull's-eye in through the open flap and get some mighty enlightening glimpses.

"It just goes to show that sex is the most exciting and predominant thought in the human mind. There I was, a small, undeveloped boy, sallying forth to glorious adventure with maybe a possum or a skunk, and still I could be interested in sex.

"At the hen-house door, which was fastened with an iron hook and a staple, Aunt Prue carefully lifted the hook and pushed the door open with the ends of the gun barrels. At the same time she nodded for me to come up alongside her and shine the light inside.

"Both of us had forgotten about Obis First Syllable of Astoria, the dog that was supposed to keep any varmints from bothering the chickens. However, he had roused from his bed on the back porch and followed us down the path. When we stopped at the hen-house door and I stepped forward, Obie lifted his nose and sniffed Aunt Prue's leg through the flap in her underwear. His nose, as cold as an icicle in Alaska, touched her leg.

"Aunt Pru jumped, let out a big yelp, and jerked both triggers. A big old coon came out the hen-house door, upset me and the lantern, and tore off down the hill with Obis First Syllable of Astoria tearing after him, barking for all he was worth."

Shawn was enjoying the story, but Rembrandt didn't crack a smile. She seldom does, no matter how hard I try to make her giggle. She had a bizarre sense of humor. Sadistic. That old yarn about a guy sliding on his bare caboose down a cellar door with nails in it is about the only one I know of that is sure to make her grin.

"When the smoke had cleared away we counted thirteen dead chickens. The charges of No. 6 drop shot had raked along the entire length of one roosting pole, tearing such big holes in some of the chickens that there was hardly anything left of them. We gathered up enough, though, that it took us till midnight to douse them in scalding water and pick and clean them.

"All but one she kept for us, Aunt Prue gave to the Old Folks Home. That's the kind of person she was, God bless her happy old soul."

I got my battered old road grip, put my lunch in it and otherwise prepared to go to work. By this time it was a quarter to five and I had to be ready to take mail into my car at a quarter past. Mentally, I ran through my list of supplies and equipment — a Foreman high-behind almost has to set up housekeeping when he goes to work: Badge, mail keys, travel commission; money, gun, watch; slips for addressing packages of letters, labels for pouches and sacks, record of pouches received or dispatched; schemes of mail distribution, schedules of mail routes, Postal Laws & Regulations; pen, pencils, forms for handling registered mail; postmarking stamp, type, ink pad — my travel-scarred old suitcase bulged.

"Don't you think you should call your mother?" Rembrandt asked.

"Guess I should, at that. Thought I'd phone her from the depot at Saganois, but The Folly may be late, the way she was running yesterday, although they might have fixed it. I'll have time now, I guess. May be able to get through right away this time of morning. And Mom's already up."

Ordinarily when an old person dies there is a routine funeral held, after which relatives and friends go on living their daily lives, wondering a bit, perhaps, how soon they themselves will pass on. Nobody is surprised, because at eighty or ninety death is expected any time. That was the way I thought it would be with Aunt Prue — but how wrong I was.

I want to say that Aunt Prudence Persnosky's death and funeral was the doggonedest "weary," as we say down in my old home country of Spunky Ridge, that I ever underwent, and that if I had known that Tuesday morning in April, 1961 what I knew later I never would have answered the phone. I would have let it ring itself out, and Mr. Stambo could have called my cousin Bonnie Dooks Stabbs in Chicago and dumped the whole business in her superexpansive lap. But how did I know but what The Folly had been annulled that day for some flimsy reason, the way the Burlington Route had been trying to convince the Interstate Commerce Commission that the jerkwater line should be discontinued because it was losing money? There was the chance that I wouldn't have had to work that Tuesday, but would get paid just the same, account I worked for the Post Office Department on an annual salary.

2 I set my grip on the floor by the kitchen door, went in the living room to the phone and placed a call to Mom down in Saganois. Listening to the message being relayed through Galesburg, Springfield and Jacksonville, I wondered if my mother would break down and take it hard when she heard about Aunt Prue's death, and guessed that she wouldn't, not for long, anyway. In a minute or so Mom answered, "Hel-lo."

My Mom makes talking on the telephone a precise rite. Her thin lips have to be pursed exactly so, and she has to be sitting in her wide-armed telephone chair complete with pencil and writing pad. I could picture her nudging her smooth gray hair up to the top of her ear with the receiver so as not to risk distortion of the words by hearing them through hair. Her soft brown eyes would be sort of raised to God, as though thanking Him for the miracle of the telephone. For Mom is old enough to have heard at her mother's knee the first telling of the amazing story of "What hath God wrought?"

"Hello, Mom, this is Boley. How you doing?"

"All right, Bolander. How are you, thataway and that?"

I had been named after a grandfather quite a few greats back, a turbaned Turk warrior who had fought around Istanbul when that city was called Constantinople—the hard word for school kids to spell. "O.K., Mom, except I just got a phone call from out in Oregon that Aunt Prue d————passed away." I had almost said died, forgetting momentarily that in Mom's language nobody ever died, only passed away.

"Oh, oh, my poor little sister!" Mom said. I could tell by her tones that she was trying to cry some but was able to squeeze out only a tear or two from each eye, the way she sounded. Mom cries easily, too, but Aunt Prue was a person over whom it was practically impossible to cry, even though she had passed away so suddenly. Every time you thought about her you recalled some silly thing she had done or said, and you had to laugh. I've seen and heard people snicker just from watching her walk or listening to her tell about the most ordinary incidents.

"How did it happen? What was she doing? How much money did she leave?"

Mom was a Dinnegan, and the Dinnegans are the type of Irishers who have had a relative, near or distant, in the thick of everything that has happened in the United States ever since Cornwallis was shelled to a cob at Yorktown. Mom didn't mean to be gossipy or greedy, but just wanted to add to her store of subjects of conversation. She had a lot of things to talk about and discussing them regularly kept her busy. One of her favorite stories concerned the first Paydoley to come to America from Turkey. His name was Theosophus and he landed at New Orleans in 1798. He was so glad to get out of Turkey, and so grateful to New Orleans for letting him come ashore, that he asked the first woman he met on Canal Street to marry him. She was a Mesquakie Indian girl named Little Bow, the daughter of Chief Settin' On A Horse Eatin' Corn, and she said yes. The chief had been sent from up around Dubuque down the Mississippi with a couple of fox hides stuffed with messages in Indian signs from various members of tribes and addressed to the French representatives of King Louis. "So you see," Mom would tell anyone, "the mail service in our family got off to an early start and is still going: Smoke signals to V-mail, when Boley was in the army, and he'll be shootin' missile mail next."

Not all the Paydoley men had made the Post Office Department a career, but a lot of them had. My Dad, Barnekus Paydoley, born in 1871, had been appointed a rural mail carrier at Saganois, in 1896, when that service was first started. That same year he married Molly Dinnegan, from Spunky Ridge, and I was born a year later: 1897, the year Mr. Winchester perfected his pump shotgun, the Model '97. The '97, with its sinister-looking hammer that lies so flat, is the only pumpgun that I can hit consistently with, and I think it must be because I was born the same year it was and have an affinity with it. The newer Model 12 is a much sleeker-looking gun, hammerless, but with a straight-stock, and I can't hit as well with it as I can with the '97, which has more of a drop at the heel, and you have to cover your target. I have a tendency to overshoot with the Model 12.

My Dad didn't last long as a rural-route man. Mom would never tell me much about this particular job he had, but Aunt Prue did. She said his Indian blood craved dilution with whisky, and as he looked more like a Turk than an Indian he could buy it. He used to carry the mail in a box buggy with a horse hitched to it. At the right front corner of the buggy box was a staff from which flew a weather flag, so the country people would know what kind of meteorology to expect, as in those days of course there were no radios or TV weather men with pointers, charts or pieces of chalk. A white flag meant fair weather, red was stormy, blue meant snow (at this point Aunt Prue usually mentioned Paul Bunyan and the year of the blue snow, when Babe, the blue ox, that was sixteen ax handles and a plug of chewing tobacco between the horns, and was so strong that he could pull anything that had an end to hitch to, was born) and so on down through the list of informative colors. About twice a week Dad would get whisky mixed with his hues and was likely to be seen going along the road flying a blue flag in June. He always delivered the mail, but couldn't be depended on to bring the right kind of weather.

He finally got so bad he had to be transferred, so he was made Post Master at Spunky Ridge, Illinois, in the heart of the Military Tract, when that place was a thriving coal-mine community with a Post Office that grossed all of $750.00 a year. Hadn't been a P.M. long when a bandit held him up one day, poking a pistol through the stamp window. Instead of raising his arms as anyone else would, Dad chounced him, and the bandit shot him right through the brisket.

I told Mom everything I had learned about Aunt Prue's death, and she said she would phone her brother, my Uncle Lanky Frank Dinnegan down in Spunky Ridge, and her two sisters Millie and Maud, who lived right there in Saganois, and anyone else she thought might be interested — which I knew included everyone in the south half of Starbuck County. "I'll call your cousin Bonnie right away, too," Mom told me. "She's all the time writing that story of hers, she can just write the obit."

Bonnie is the daughter of Uncle Parley Dooks and Aunt Maud. Bonnie and I might have married if we hadn't been cousins, because we were usually fighting at the family reunions we went to when we were kids, and even yet I didn't like her any too well. But I married Rembrandt Foster, glory be, and Bonnie married a Fancy Dan house-to-house collector of insurance premiums named Charles Willard Stabbs, who had callouses on his knuckles from knocking on doors, and now they had six children and eight grandchildren. Brandy and I have only three and six, not counting those in sight, respectively, so I guess everything turned out for the progenitive best, after all. Bonnie was a type of nincompoop. She thought she could splatter pretty hard against the ground, no matter in what field she squatted, but particularly in the artistic areas, and more particularly in the realm of writing. She also had her palms read regularly, as well as her soles.

"When you talk to Bonnie," I told Mom, "tell her the lawyer found Aunt Prue's will but hadn't opened it yet. That will give her something to think about."

The feeling that existed between Bonnie and me can be described as armed and wary neutrality. We were Aunt Prue's favorite relatives, I because I had a government job, which in Aunt Prue's patriotic opinion was quite an honor; and Bonnie because ever since she had left high school she had been trying to write a story, and this appealed to the artist in Aunt Prue. Cousin Bonnie and I probably would inherit the bulk of our aunt's estate.

For forty years Bonnie had been writing on a story called "*Lost Moments*." It was a tender love story about two boys named Jack and Henry, and a girl named June. Bonnie had written it in short-short-story form, short-story form, long-story form, and had tried sev-

eral times to make a novel out of it. Then she had made
it into a stage-acting play, as well as a radio play. At
the funeral she told me she was going to make a tele-
vison show out of it.

"If you figure on having Bonnie write the obit," I
told Mom, "you better get her started on it right away.
Because if she doesn't work any faster on it than she
does on *Lost Moments* she won't have it done anyway
near in time for the funeral."

"I'll call her right away and get her started on it.
You'll be down to help make the funeral arrangements, you and Rembrandt and Shawn, that away and
that, won't you?"

"I'll work today and lay off the rest of the week. Can't
get a substitute to run for me today—too short notice.
I just got this call about half an hour ago. We'll be
down late tonight or the first thing tomorrow morning
unless I call you."

"I'll go ahead and get as much done as I can."

"O.K. Goodby."

"Goodby."

I knew Mom would take care of a lot of details. She
has been a widow for so many years that she is used
to doing things by herself. Ask people who know Mrs.
Molly Paydoley and they will tell you that she is a
woman who gets things done. Give her something to
worry about and she is at her happiest and most efficient. At eighty-five she has helped out at so many funerals of friends and relatives that she was particularly good at handling them. She had an uncanny
knack of knowing before hand who was going to break
down and take it hard and go on fit to kill, and she
would be ready with handkerchiefs and camphor to dry
their tears, comfort them and revive the fainty.

"The Lord giveth and He taketh away," Mom would
tell them, "and they ain't nothin' fairer than that!"

3 We live in the country on four acres of brush-and-gully land that doesn't have a level spot on it, which gives Rembrandt and me the excuse not to raise even a garden. We like to live in the country but we don't like to farm. It is about five miles from our house to the depot at Windfall.

"Now that I'm up," Shawn said, "I'll drive you to work, and meet you tonight when you get in. Besides, I want to talk to you." She slipped a red housecoat on over her pajamas."

The morning was fresh, clear and balmy, and quite a few farmers were already out doing their chores and keeping an eye out for Sputnik, Explorer, Vanguard or whatever the current satellite was named, sometimes visible just before dawn, when we drove out the lane onto the pavement. Whenever Shawn contrives to drive me to or from work I know I'm in for a few minutes of interesting father-daughter talk. I've learned more about the vagaries of womankind from Shawn and those rides than I ever learned from Rembrandt or Mom. She began by asking, "Should we let Roman and Fred know about Aunt Prue?"

Roman and Fred are her brothers. Roman lives on the east coast and Fred on the west. The siblings never bicker, thanks to distance, and are always glad to see one another.

"Might send them wires, but I don't think they'll come. Neither of them has seen Aunt Prue for years, and wouldn't know her if they did. Do you intend to go to the funeral?"

"I don't think so."

"Couldn't you get somebody to work for you long enough so you could drive your old clunker down just for the funeral? It would look better. Rem and I will

probably have to stay a day or two, but you wouldn't."
Shawn teaches Physical Education at the Windfall
YWCA. "You wouldn't have to miss but about one
date." I glanced sideways at her. "Or how hairy is the
guy you're interested in this month?"

Shawn belongs to what she calls a Love Of The
Month Club, and in its colorful slang men are rated
hairy, hairier, hairiest and whiskers-to-their-eyes.

"He's getting hairier all the time, but he's not a
Samson and is still on probation."

"Who is he?"

"Bill Tarsevik. Tall, blonde and sunburned. He's the
farm boy you met last fall when you hunted quail on
his Dad's farm. His Dad wants to retire and go to Florida and leave the farm to him."

"More Cadillacs in the corn than anywhere else,
Time magazine says. Relatively speaking, that is."

"And milking is easy to learn — like putting on tight
gloves, only you strip them off."

"Is he ready for the postmark test? You might have
him out to the house some time and we'll give him the
works."

"I tested him myself the other night when you and
Mom went to the movies. He set up Lulu, Florida; Cut
Off, Louisana; Herron, Michigan; and Peterman, Alagama!"

"Gee whiz!"

"That's what I thought, too. That's what I want to
talk to you about."

"I wouldn't bother with him seriously. He's either a
baby-hater or a sadist — one of those guys who gets a
kick out of hurting or embarrassing people."

"I just wanted you to verify my analysis."

"If he's anything like his old man he's a pretty good
farmer," I said helpfully. "The buildings were all in
good shape, no machinery parked in the open, no weeds

along fences—no quail either, there wasn't any place for them to hide. Have you been out there?"

"Oh, yes. I like his mother. But I saw a big armchair with a pair of house slippers beside it on the floor and the morning newspaper on a stand alongside. It was late afternoon and the paper hadn't been opened yet. That told me a lot. I don't know whether Bill Tarsevik has recovered enough from that Old World routine of existence or not: Monday wash, Tuesday iron and so forth." Shawn sighed and I swallowed. "However," she continued, "the idea of clipping hair out of his ears doesn't make me shudder. But a girl has to take many facts and hunches into consideration. In a lot of ways Mrs. Tarsevik gave me the impression that she was another Balkan domestic farm animal."

"Being a farmer, Bill could have used Cucumber, West Virginia after Cut Off and Herron, at least. Or was it in the box of nouns—no, I guess I threw my Cucumber away, it was so worn out and curled—I'll have to write for a new one. I don't know. Lulu didn't have to mutilate her man."

"Do you suppose Bill's had bad luck with some girl and craves revenge?"

Before I could answer the car swung around a curve and we saw the stalled truck on the shoulder of the road. It was a big flat-bed truck with three logs chained on it. Red warning flares burned front and rear and on the side next to the pavement. A husky young bareheaded chap in coveralls and lumberman's pacs waved a red five-gallon gasoline can at us. Shawn slowed the car and rolled the window down.

"So I run out of gas," the guy said. "So I think I'm unlucky. So a beautiful young virgin comes along at five in the morning. She takes me to get gas and brings me back. So it is the luckiest day of my life."

"See here, Mister—" I began.

"Get in," Shawn said, stifling a yawn. She reached back and unlocked the rear door.

"I'm Bill Dugan," the guy said. "Lumber. Mostly railroad ties."

"Not too glad to meet you, Mr. Dugan," Shawn said.

"My name's Paydoley," I said.

It was too awkward to shake hands in the car, so we didn't. I looked at Shawn and wondered if I should say anything. Her body was rigid, her usually composed face strained, and her hands gripped the wheel until her knuckles showed a paler pink than her fingers. Shawn ordinarily drives with the relaxed ease of a kitty basking in the sun.

"This is my daughter, Shawn."

Shawn turned her head and nodded. Dugan was hunched forward, and his close-shaved, sun-tanned face was closer than she expected it to be. The right front wheel ran off the slab, and the car slowed before it edged back on.

Mr. Dugan remained silent until the sensible maneuver was completed, then said, "Hello, Shawn. Don't mind that. All lady-girls get flustered when I get as close to them as I am to you."

"Phenomenal," Shawn said, "as well as astonishing. Also very tiresome."

"If we meet a car I promise to get clear back in the corner of the seat."

"Please do — or get out."

Listening to such banal banter makes me uncomfortable. "Those were walnut logs, weren't they?" I said. "You don't make railroad ties out of black walnut, do you?"

"No. I'm taking them to the gunstock factory out on the west edge of town."

"The one that burned?"

"The guy's starting up again."

Mr. Dugan and I talked gunstocks. I told him how surprised I was when I was in the army in 1942 and found Made In Windfall stamped on the stock of my rifle. He listened politely and — looking at my wrinkled skin and gray hair — unbelievably.

When we deposited Mr. Dugan at the truck stop on Madison Road he said, "Thank you kindly, Mr. Paydoley. Thank you, too, Shawn, bless your heart. How long before you get back? In that slinky and domestic-looking housecoat you can't be going far. To the depot?"

Shawn nodded miserably.

"Ten minutes?" Dugan said brightly.

Again Shawn nodded.

"Bad old tongue-loving cat."

We were within a few blocks of the depot and Shawn hadn't said a word about the beauty and silence of the new day, housewives we could see through kitchen windows getting breakfasts, the obvious and appalling need for garages, or what a lousy job I had that I had to get up at such an inhuman hour. "What's the matter?" I asked. "Cutworms in the corn?"

"No," she said meaningly. "Borers."

I chuckled my appreciation of the corny corn-borer gag, so common in the middle west, the welfare of which depended a great deal on the control of the grain-destroying insect. "Better take Summer Street home. You really don't want to go back past the truck stop, do you?"

"I should say not! Did you ever see a crew-cut grow so low on a forehead?"

"Didn't notice. You're not under any real obligation to haul him back, you know — this time of night and everything. You better take Summer Street home."

"I wouldn't think of going back and maybe having to wrestle with him."

"He won't have to wait long. Somebody will haul him back."

I wasn't worried about Shawn being able to take care of herself. I had taught her all the crotch-kicks, knee-lifts, neck-twists and other ways and means of maiming or killing men that the army had taught me, but there wasn't any use in taking unnecessary risks.

At the depot I got out, took my grip, and went to work. Steve Medill was on duty at the Mail Transfer Office, which is a cubbyhole set up in every railroad station where the mail transfer from one form of transportation to another, or from one train to another, is of sufficient quantity to warrant special supervision. Steve sat at his dingy desk working on a stack of space requests. One of a Transfer Clerks' duties is to ascertain the amount of space needed in a train to haul mail. Counting both sides of a storage car, he figures sixteen or eighteen sacks to the foot, depending on the vagaries of the Post Office Department, and fills out the space-request forms accordingly. The requests act as vouchers and are handed to the conductor or baggageman, who turns them in at the end of the run so the railroad company can collect its mail revenue.

Steve was not a mine-run mail-car highbehind because he never had to get out and bark his shins up and down the road in a bucking, swaying mail car— and stoop to trade outgoing mail for incoming at every station. Transfer Clerks are of course called Tom Cats.

"Good morning, Steve," I said. "Say, Steve, get a sub for me the rest of the week, can you? I have to go to a funeral down at Saganois. My aunt."

Steve's bulging blue eyes grew solemn. It was his job to collect money for flowers whenever any clerk or a member of his family died, and he had a special look of sympathy that he hung on his face for the occasion. "You'll want flowers?"

"She's only my aunt, but we kicked in for a bouquet for Bob Grant's mother-in-law awhile back, so I guess it will be all right. Whatever the boys want to do."

"Where should the flowers be sent?"

"I'll have to let you know about that later. You see, she died out in Oregon and we don't know yet whether she will be shipped here or to Saganois. I can let you know for sure about the flowers when I get in tonight. You can get a sub for me, can't you?"

"I think so. Scotty isn't working this week."

Gilbert Scott was a highbehind substitute. He was an ex-serviceman who had taken the Civil Service examination for postal transportation clerk, and by adding the veteran's automatic five percent to his grade had made 102. That was in 1953, and he had been appointed immediately. However, here eight years later he was still a sub. So many trains had been removed because of competition from other forms of mail transportation that he was farther away from a regular job than he was when he started. He would have resigned long ago but didn't want to lose his seniority. Including his military service, he had ten years Civil Service seniority and was steadily building up his retirement annuity.

"You get hold of Scotty then, and I'll write the office and fix up my leave."

The United States Postal Transportaion Service is divided into divisions for administrative purposes, and each division is sub-divided into districts. My district office is in Anniston; and my District Superintendent is Mr. George Gregory Mansfield, a dapper, precise little man with political connections extending all the way to Washington. Each district has on its roster one substitute for every six or eight clerks, to take care of vacations, sick leave and such, and these subs are scattered over the district. It was fortunate for me that

Sub Scott lived at Windfall.

"O.K.," Steve said. "You want your registers now?"

Another job of a Tom Cat is handling registered mail. Records have to be kept on registers, and hand-to-hand receipt obtained whenever possible. Most of them are counted, and then billed in bulk, but if any registered piece of mail has a blue pencil check-mark on it, its number and office of origin has to be recorded, for the mark indicates more than nominal value.

"Might as well. Is The Folly spotted yet?"

In the mail-sorting room outside the door of the Transfer Office I heard a mail-handler yell, "All ready for the Saganois," and I knew my train had been brought up from the roundhouse and was ready to take on mail, express and perhaps a bit of baggage.

I signed for sixteen registered letters, two white canvas sacks of slot-machine money and a package of tickets for the Decoration Day races at Indianapolis, stowed them in a mail sack, and lugged them and my grip down the platform to The Folly.

The Folly is a snorting little gasoline-electric, one-car train, seventy feet long. From the rear she looks like an ordinary railway passenger coach, but from the front she looks like a Mardi Gras float. The first ten feet of her, which is the engine room, is painted stop-light red with a border of brilliant yellow. Three exhaust pipes sticking up through the roof belch smoke and flame and gas fumes when she is underway, and the gases seep back through the train and give people headaches. Her Cyclopean eye swivels sickeningly in its socket.

Next to the engine room is the fifteen-foot mail compartment, fitted with letter case with work table, pouch and sack rack with another table, and upright iron stanchions that separate the limited storage space into still smaller spaces. There is a tank of drinking water, one of wash water, a basin, and a rail-painting toilet. Iron doors form a firewall between the mail compartment and the engine room, and there is a sliding door on each side.

To the rear of the mail section is thirty feet devoted to express and baggage; with the passenger compartment making up the rear fifteen feet of the train.

I climbed into the mail section, switched on the lights, and loaded on the pouches, sacks and outside parcels. Then I dressed the racks, and fiddled the address slips for the packages of letters I would later tie out of the case into their respective pigeonholes. I changed the date and train number on my iron postmarking stamp so that it read "Windfall & Saganois R.P.O., Tr. 176, April 12, 1961." I was now ready to stamp a neat, round black postmark on any first-class mail that might be posted by the public in the slot marked LETTERS that was cut in each side of the car.

These postmarks of Railway Post Offices are in themselves desirable items to collectors. So many trains have been discontinued in recent years that the slightest rumor of a line's removal deluges its mail cars with requests for last-trip postmarks.

I labeled the pouches and sacks and started throwing mail. The Folly is a one-man run and I have to do everything myself. I stooped to take in more mail as it arrived from connecting lines, stooped to lift bags of mail onto the work table, stooped to retrieve a misthrown piece of mail. Sometimes I even stooped backwards. By now it was six oclock and the train was due out at six-thirty.

Highbehinds work against time always. If the train runs faster than scheduled and time is made up, so does the work have to be made up. Between stations at least two letters have to be distributed to every click of the rails, no matter what speed the train is making.

The mail rolled in and I kept hashing away at it. I was so busy that I didn't notice the main-line train from Chicago was in until its disembarking passengers began to stream across the station platform. Then somebody swung up into the open door of my mail car, banged his head, and greeted, "Hello, there, Mr. Paydoley."

I peered over the top of my glasses. "Tarsevik, isn't it?"

"Yeah. Though I'd come over and say hello." He was a pleasant-faced boy, sun burned and wind tanned, and apparently never wore a hat or cap. He had clear blue eyes and a roach of hair the color of honey. In spite of the painful bump at which he rubbed — I've seen guys knock themselves out swinging up against a mail-car's safety bar before a warning could be yelled — he grinned.

"Glad to see you," I said. "And excuse me for not seeing you in time to holler. How's everything in Chicago?"

"Good. Sold all my hogs yesterday. Twenty-eight thousand dollars."

"You sold twenty-eight thousand dollars worth of hogs?"

"Sure did."

I knew ninety percent of thereabouts of the middle west's corn crop stayed on the farms and was fed to livestock, but I didn't realize the business made money like that. No wonder *Time* magazine said there were more Cadillacs in the corn than anywhere else. And this was the young man Shawn said was getting hairier all the time.

"How's Shawn?"

I wondered if Shawn had heeded my advice not to go home past the truck stop, but I had been so busy that I hadn't had time to call home from the Transfer Office, as I sometimes do, and learn if she got home all right. "Fine," I said. "She brought me to work this morning."

"I love Shawn," Tarsevik said, just like that. "I want to marry her. I'd like to know how you feel about the idea."

Of all the men who had proposed marriage to Shawn in the five years since she was seventeen, when she told Rembrandt and me about the first one, this Tarsevik guy was the only one who had said anything to me about the subject. I felt foolishly flattered. "Suits me fine, Bill. And I think it's mighty nice of you to ask me. Most guys wouldn't bother."

I thought of the brash young man who had run out of gas: Another guy named Bill. Bill Dugan. He gave me the impression that he wouldn't think of asking a girl's father if he could marry his daughter.

"Then it doesn't make any difference to you that I'm of Magyar descent? A Hunky?"

"Not a bit. I'm a Turk myself. On top of that I'm a hillbilly. We Hunkies and hillbilly Turks have done as much as any bunch to build up this country, I guess. We don't have to be ashamed. Besides, anybody who can raise twenty-eight thousand dollars worth of hogs a year can certainly support a wife. That's five times as much money as I ever made. Have you asked Shawn?"

"Not yet, but I will."

"She's a fine girl, Bill. Rembrandt and I have taken a lot of pains to bring her up right. And I mean *pains*. The best thing I can say about Shawn is that she's just like her mother—especially in looks."

I would have qualified my comparison of Shawn to Rem a bit more, but just then Wild Ike Highspeed Skaderight, the engineer, started The Folly's big six-cylinder Buda motor to warm it up before leaving town. Its cylinders are as big as gallon buckets, each one has four sparkplugs, and its roar made any more talk impossible.

Tarsevik climed down out of the doorway. "Goodby, Mr. Paydoley," he yelled. "Thanks."

"Take it easy, Bill. And good luck."

I had lost four or five minutes talking to the young man, and when we left town I was that much behind in my work. We were at Vinton, half way over the run, before I caught up. However, by working the mail marked No. 1 — which all goes to the close-in stations unless fellow distributors make errors of omission or commission — I didn't carry any mail by. In the Postal Transportation Service it is an unpardonable sin to carry mail by, and clerks will sweat blood and miss lunch to keep from doing it.

Vinton is at the north edge of the Spunky Ridge country. South of Vinton the rails snake up and down and around the prongs and pinnacles of Starbuck County, through thick brush and across deep gullies, until they emerge at Saganois, the outward terminus of the line, on the Saganois River.

The Folly pike is a hundred and ten miles long, and with all the flag stops, switchbacks, running in reverse up stub tracks to reach the hamlets scattered throughout the hills, it takes five hours to make the trip, one way. Thus the weeks I am on duty I put in about twelve hours a day, counting the advance work that has to be done before the train leaves town. That is why I work only every other week. Besides, barking shins every day on The Folly would poop a giant, not to mention all the overtime the government, already pressing hard against the national debt ceiling, would have to pay me.

No railroad should ever have been built down

through the rugged Spunky Ridge country, which is the for northeast end of the Ozarks that took a running jump and landed across the Mississippi. The tiny communities of Starbuck County—Sny Magrew, Limberswitch, Turtle Holler, Puckerbrush and Spunky Ridge —were not big enough to support a railroad. Moreover, the rough terrain and the south-or-sideways squirmings of the roadbed prevents anything resembling efficient operation of the line.

Back in the 1860's, however, when Corny Vanderbilt, Jim Hill and other railraod magantes were laying rails all over America, a charter was granted to build a line from Windfall to Sagnois. Dan Webster himself prepared the charter and brought it out from Boston. Dan was a close friend of John Forbes, who together with Jim Joy and John Brooks formed the combine that developed the great Burlington Route railsystem, of which The Folly is a part.

Almost from the start the little train, drawn by a wood-burning steam locomotive with a high flaring smokestack in those early days, was nicknamed The Folly. America bought Alaska from Russ about the time the line was built, and as the deal was called by many "Seward's Folly"—Bill Seward, the man who engineered the deal, being our Secretary Of State at the time—the term "Folly" was apt to be applied to any bad business venture. At first the line paid its way and more, as any pioneering American business usually does. Then as other forms of more efficient transportation were developed The Folly began to lose out to competition, just as out big railroads are doing today, except not on so large a scale. Annually for the last thirty years The Folly had lost money. It would have been discontinued long ago but for a benevolent management that understood the affection the Spunky Ridge people had for their train. The hillbillies treated The Folly as they would treat a gentle loving old grandmother who had outlived her usefulness but who was still loved, respected and tolerated—a nice old thing to have around.

We pulled into Saganois on time at eleven-thirty. I don't have time to go see my mother, because she lives out at the edge of town, and I have to get back to work on the return trip in less than an hour. I call her on the phone every day, and when I talked to her this Tuesday she said she was working hard on getting things done.

"I called Millie and Maud and Frank and Bonnie," Mom said. "And Bonnie was to get to work on the obit right away. She's going to work on it on the way down here on the train, too. She'll be down tomorrow, I told her quite a few things she could put in the obit, about the time Prue paid five dollars for a fiddle and sold it for five thousand because it was such a fine fiddle, and about the time she—"

"Did you get a preacher?"

"No. I and Millie and Maud and Frank thought we'd wait till we all got together, thataway and that, before we decided about a preacher. Sister Prue wasn't much for religion."

"Remember the time she called Reverend Reed a salvation peddler and accused him of selling salvation by the sack?"

Mom laughed. She remembered, all right. She was with Aunt Prue when it happened, which was long before I was born—in fact, Mom and Dad hadn't met yet. The two girls had run away from home to find jobs, and my old Grandfather Dinnegan and Reverend Reed had located them over in Missouri and had gone to bring them back. They got my mother, all right, and would have got Aunt Prue, too, I guess, the way Mom always told the story, but Reverend Reed got to preaching a little too hard at her and she broke loose and got away. Didn't show up for several years.

"By the way, how old was she?"

"She's a year and a half older than I am. She was born in 1874. April Fool day."

"The lawyer out in Oregon wants to know. I couldn't remember whether she was older than you or not. I'll send the lawyer a telegram."

"She married Phineas in 1895, the year Papa passed away."

Aunt Prue had met Phineas Persnosky when they were both house gamblers on a Mississippi River packet boat called the *Prairie Belle*. Aunt Prue ran the poker game and Uncle Phin was a crap-table croupier. They got to gambling just between themselves, Aunt Prue said, and she won all of Uncle Phin's money, then won him. He looked a good deal like the Jack of Hearts: Wore his hair long and had only one eye. He died over in India in 1910; just wore himself out trying to keep up with his wife.

"What else have you done?"

"Fixin' things to eat. I guess everybody will come out here after the funeral, and I thought maybe they'd like a bite before they started home."

That was like my Mom, always concerned with the welfare of people. Getting together for a bite to eat after a funeral is a Spunky Ridge custom that Mom has been familiar with all her life. For in Mom's day roads or weather were apt to be so bad that funerals sometimes lasted two or three days.

"You folks will be down tonight, won't you?" Mom asked.

"Either tonight or first thing in the morning. If the train gets in on time we might be down tonight."

When I got back to the mail car, Wild Ike Highspeed Skaderight, the engineer, and old man Skates, the combination conductor, brakeman and baggageman, were already eating their lunch on the work table by the letter case. We all eat together in the mail compartment because it is handy to the tank of drinking water.

"Right on time today," Lou Skates said in his whiny voice. "I guess they fixed the trickle valve." He was a thin, shaky-jointed old fellow, away past the retirement age, but kept begging the railroad company to let him stay on the job because he wouldn't know what to do with himself if he retired.

Straggly gray hair stuck out from under his conductor's cap, which was the only part of the trainman's uniform he wore, his other jobs being of far more importance than presenting a remote and austere appearance, and condescending to give the correct railroad time. For The Folly carried more livestock, crates of eggs, chicken coops and milk cans than passengers; and although Mr. Skates carried a ticket punch in the pocket of the vest he wore under his bib overalls, he didn't have much use for it. Nobody rode The Folly much any more except people too old to drive cars, and school teachers on Monday mornings and Friday nights.

"She worked all right, anyway, this morning," Skaderight said. "I been puttin' that trickle valve on my work sheet ever' night for two weeks, so I guess maybe they got around to fixin' it."

Wild Ike Highspeed Skaderight was a bulky, swaggering, old-time engineer, as impertinent and bombastic as any trainmen of the days when railraods had no competition could get. At sixty-five he had fifty years of service, and in his smug and prideful life had waved condescendingly from the throne of his jouncing locomotive at many buggies, wagons and automobiles stuck in mud roads that paralelled the rails.

"In 1923," Lou Skates mused, "the year I took that trip out to Seattle, Washington and down through Californy and back we was on time ever' station all but one. And do you know why we was late at that one station?"

There was no subject on which Highspeed was not an authority. "Yeah," he said. "Bad trickle valve."

"That's right. It kept stickin'."

I never could understand why so many trainmen insist on calling the triple valve on the Westinghouse railroad air brake a trickle valve, but they do. However, everybody knows what they mean. The one on The Folly had been acting up for some time. We would be roller-skating along nicely, maybe coasting down grade, and Ike would want to slow down a bit. He would ease a little air on and sometimes the brakes would take hold and sometimes they wouldn't. And once, the week before, when Joe Moller, the clerk who runs opposite me, was on, the brakes grabbed so suddenly that all the letters flew out of their pigeonholes and Joe piled up against the engine-room firewall and hurt his toe.

By the time old man Skates finished telling about the trip he had made in 1923, which was the only time Lou had ever been out of Illinois; and Wild Ike had gone into details about his "herny" operation and his "prostrate" gland trouble, it was time to go to work again. I went over to the depot to send a telegram to Mr. Stambo about how old Aunt Prue was, and while I was at it I called Mr. Parker at the funeral home. He told me he had just received a wire that Aunt Prue was on her way and would arrive Friday afternoon on the 1:33 train from St. Louis.

"Gee whiz!" I thought, "Friday afternoon. And here it was Tuesday afternoon already."

4 When The Folly got back to Windfall, Rembrandt was waiting for me in the car. She was all dressed up and I knew she was ready to take off for Saganois. unloaded the mail, delivered my registers to the Transfer Office, and told Steve Medill to send the flowers to Saganois.

The first thing I said to Rembrandt was, "Did Shawn get back home this morning all right?"

"I guess so," Rem said. "I went back to bed but I heard her come in. And at breakfast she didn't say anything. Why?"

"I just wondered. Some guy ran out of gas on Madison Avenue this morning and we hauled him in to the truck stop. He wanted Shawn to haul him back on her way home, but I told her to go out Summer Street home, so I guess she did. She didn't say anything about it, huh?"

"No. About all she said was she wouldn't be home for supper; so we might as well go down to Saganois tonight. She said she had a date with Bill."

"Did she say she would try to make it to the funeral?"

"I think she's planning on it—she's not so callous or selfish or hardboiled as she seems about things like funerals. Said she would have to have a little work done on the Clunker first—points and plugs and something else. I think she'll be there. When do you think the funeral will be? We'll have to call her and let her know."

"Friday, I imagine. And Friday is a good day for funerals. Jesus, you know."

"Do you want to leave now? We could eat supper at Vinton. I brought your good clothes."

"Did you bring a belt and necktie?"

"Yes." she grinned.

Rembrandt usually forgets belt and necktie when she packs my grip, like when I have to go to Anniston for my regular spring and fall examinations, but makes up for them on underwear and handkerchiefs. I bet I own fifty belts and neckties that I've had to buy out of town. I think sometimes that Brandy has some obscure wife's complex that makes her want me to appear sloppily dressed, in startling contrast to her own always neat appearance.

"Might as well take off," I said, "Mom's looking for us."

It is 125 miles from Windfall down to Saganois if you stay on the pavement, which edges around the roughest part of the Spunky Ridge country and crosses the river at Sny Magrew, the first station out of Saganois on The Folly line. The trip takes about three hours, counting coffee-stops and rest-rooms. Rembrandt and I rolled along and thought how fortunate we were that we had been married forty-three years almost and brought up three kids without having any funerals in our family. Sometimes we can drive for miles, thinking about things like that, looking back on all the experiences, good and bad, that we have shared, and never say a word. But at the same time somehow Brandy knows what I am thinking about, and I sense what is on her mind. This time, however, our minds were far apart.

"It's too bad Aunt Prue hated people," Rembrandt

said.

I looked across at her. Her face was set in deep thought. Brandy has great dignity. Once when we lived in town she was waiting at the street corner in front of the house for a bus to take her shopping. The curb was icy, and just as she went to step into the bus her foot slid out from under her and she sat down flat on her caboose. She was so humiliated that she scrambled up, turned around and came back into the house and called a taxicab. I was watching out the upstairs window and saw the whole thing.

"She didn't hate people," I said. "She had the keenest sense of humor of anyone I ever saw—even if women are not supposed to have a sense of humor. You can't see fun in everything like she did and hate people." Rembrandt sure has some cockeyed ideas.

"Most of her humor was based on sacrilege, contempt, sarcasm or vulgarity. A great deal of it was downright insulting. It was not true humor."

"I think I know what you're driving at: What she said about me and my job."

"That's an excellent example."

I knew what Brandy meant. Aunt Prue used to drop in on us every year or two. She never stayed long, but after she left it was a week before our household recovered from her merry, sharp-shinned philosophy and returned to normal. And once she told me that being the kind of guy I was, I was lucky to be hiding behind the protecting skirts of a government job. She said I never would be able to make as much money in a non-governmental job as I made in the Civil Service; said I couldn't hold my own in give-and-take, aggressive business competition; said people like me should get jobs like I had or else go into military service and stay there. If she had told me that when I was in my twenties I would have resented it, but now I realized it was the truth.

"Well," I said slowly," Aunt Prue was right. When you get older you come cleaner and more honest with yourself. I've never made much money. I'm just not one of those people who can make a lot of money."

"You could if you really wanted to, but you always have too many other things to do: Books to read, game to hunt, fish to catch; and fooling around with those silly postmarks."

"Jeff Lay Lulu on the High Couch?" I snickered.

"See! There you go. You have a good mind, but see how it works. Nothing practical."

"Maybe Aunt Prue will leave me some money in her will. Give me a start. Maybe I can take the money and fix up the basement so we can raise Morel mushrooms in it and harvest twenty-five pounds of them every morning and haul them to town and sell them for a dollar a pound."

"You see, Boley, you're hopeless. You can't even imagine a really good business — one, for instance, that has a thousand-dollar electric bill every month. Besides, I don't think she had much money. Money didn't mean any more to her than it does to you — but for a different reason: because she made it so easily. No matter where she was or what she did, money circulated around her on a sort of endless belt, and all she had to do was reach out and take what she wanted."

It was true. Aunt Prue made money but gave most of it away. She made a small fortune running the poker game on packet boats, and another when she took Uncle Phin with her to the Klondike in 1898 and ran a gambling house there for awhile. It was in the Klondike that she lost the tip of her middle finger on her left hand. Said she wore it off rubbing out chalk marks playing Seven Up, but Uncle Phin told me once she lost it in a knife fight.

I never knew Uncle Phin very well. He died when I was still a kid; died over in India, after he and Aunt Prue sold their Spunky Ridge hill farm and went traveling with a magician show that made an elephant disappear right off the stage. That was once when Aunt Prue didn't have much money, because she told how it took nearly all she had to bring Uncle Phin back to Spunky Ridge and bury him. She said she got a tape line and a globe, and measured, and if Phin had died a quarter of an inch east or west from where he passed away he would have been closer home.

Uncle Phineas Persnosky reminded me of an amateur hunter following his guide, the way he tried to keep up with Aunt Prue: The brush was thick, the going uncertain, and a bear or something might leap out and chounce him if he should fall too far behind. He was a big man, but fragile. Played the accordian, but only a little while at a time because his arms got tired. Aunt Prue had met him in Cincinnati, which was the winter quarters of the *Prairie Belle,* and talked him into taking the gambling job on the boat, running the craps table.

One time, long after Brandy and I were married, Aunt Prue was visiting us. The kids had all gone to bed, and the three of us were sitting out in the yard drinking beer. It was a warm summer eveining, and a half moon was swinging up across the southern sky. Katydids chorused in our cedar trees, crickets chirped in the dewy bluegrass, and Aunt Prue grew reminiscent:

"I'd heard about Phineas Persnosky before I met him and the name fascinated me. I used to whisper 'Mrs. Prudence Persnosky' to myself, and write it on things. He came from a long line of Persnoskys. His father was the leader of a famous troop of Russian Cossacks that rode in Buffalo Bill's Wild West show. He still had his father's fur hat. I buried it with him.

"He was a flock-shooter with the ladies—never was satisfied to shoot just one at a time. When I asked him to marry me so I could raise a family he said he was not the man for me, said he had probably slept with every woman in Cincinnati, and that I'd better marry somebody else.

"I just told him I loved him, and I didn't care if he *had* slept with every woman in Cincinnati—Cincinnati ain't so big."

"He was quite a fisherman, wasn't he?" I asked.

Aunt Prue pointed her beer schooner down at the damp grass and said solemnly and proudly, "He could catch fish right out there if everyone kept quiet."

It was easy to imagine Aunt Prue carrying Uncle Phin off to her bed. She was a tall slender red-haired woman with wiry muscles and the energy of a steam engine. Instead of walking she sort of bounced. She had a shape that stopped men in their tracks—and a face that started them walking hastily again. Her face looked as though it might have been poured, like concrete, and the forms had slipped. Moreover, it was of a brownish, spit-quick color.

There was enough skin on her face for two faces, which of course made for lots of wrinkes. She had what is known in medical language as a "leonine skin." It was soft as silk, but there was too much of it. She said she once rented her face as a model for Halloween masks.

Rembrandt and I were still talking about Aunt Prue when we pulled into the Driv-In Diner at Vinton for supper. We can't afford to eat out very often, this was a treat for Rem, and she was in talkative high spirits. She said, "Aunt Prue had everything she wanted except one thing."

"What?"

"A child. She wanted a family. That's why she hated people. She tried to compensate for the children she never had by hating people and ridiculing them."

"I guess she was a barren doe, all right; and after Uncle Phin died she sure talked enough about artificial insemination. But she was too far ahead of the times, and only shocked people. Nobody would think anything unusual about such a thing nowadays, even if she advertised in the newspapers."

"She only talked like that because she wanted a man," psychologist Rem said. "She could do that without being considered immoral."

"You never liked her much, did you?"

"On the contrary, I did. I admired her a great deal, mostly for her ability to do anything well. That time she was in Denver and saw that display in a department store window and went in and told the manager she could arrange it much better. He told her to go ahead, and she did and won first prize that Christmas."

"She did, at that. And look at that ant business she had down in Texas for awhile: Bred ants and sold them by the bushel to every zoo in the country that had an anteater — sold to laboratories, too. She was a great old girl. Pawky."

"She was something of a witch, too. She even looked a little like the popular conception of a witch — a happy, grinning one."

Aunt Prue had a slender face, and the outside crinkles of her eyes slanted upward. Her chin was a little pointed, too, and so was her nose. Each had a slight tendency to slope toward the other, and after she got older and had to wear false teeth, whenever she took them out her nose and chin came alarmingly close to touching.

"I never saw her riding a broom," I said wittily.

"All the same, there was something witchlike about

her, something supernatural. I think you'll agree with me on that before the funeral is over. It's something that we can't understand. I believe Aunt Prue is laughing at all of us right now, thinking about all the trouble she caused by dying the way she did, away out there in Oregon."

5 The first thing Rembrandt and I noticed when we stopped in front of Mom's big house was the funeral wreath hanging on the knob of the front door. The shades were up, and through the windows we could see the current darling of American grandmas on the television set.

"I see Mom's been getting things done, all right," I said. "I wouldn't have thought about a wreath."

"She probably hasn't stopped working since you called her this morning. I don't see how she does it."

"That looks like Cousin Manford's car. Probably they're all in there making plans."

"I hope she has that foul-mouthed parrot's cage covered for the night."

My Mom loves birds and has half a dozen cages of canaries and parakeets, besides a cantankerous red-and-green parrot named Belshazzar that keeps yelling over and over, "Somebody-at-the-door," with epithets, every time the doorbell or telephone rings.

Mom had been watching for us. She opened the door, kissed Brandy and me, and as usual started talking a blue streak. "Thanks for the tulip bulbs, Rembrandt, I was real glad to get them, don't know why they didn't turn out any better than they did—I goofted, I guess. And I thought I'd have some glads in bloom by this time, they come up nice and tall but I can't see any buds on 'em any place, so what I think happened is, I bet the glad potatoes were just dug up and put in the bags and sold, they didn't get to rest like they do at home, either that or I goofted on them, too."

By switching the subject of conversation, sometimes Mom can be slowed down or even completely stopped for a moment or two. I nodded out the window at the brilliantly lighted house-trailer camp that had sprouted across the street a couple of years ago, the occupants of which were an endless source of interest to Mom. "How's everything going with the trailerites?"

"Them new people from Kentucky moved out so I don't have to look at them two old trailers any more — Oh, I mean three old trailers, 'cause Potts' old one burned up. Got a red trailer in its place. Mr. Boomershine has a new friend now, a lady lives next to her in a real small trailer and shakes like the dickens, lame in one leg and is full of "Yessums," so I'm real glad them two got together, only thing is this one is only sixty-five — looks a lot older — but maybe she had a hard time in her young days, poor soul. Mrs. Boomershine has to still set with the hot-water bottle on her ankle — it used to be the ice bag on her leg."

Desperately I cut in, "How are the birds?"

"Mrs. Boomershine give me the female chartreuse, so I got her in the cage with my green one, but for what, I don't know really — see if we get some young ones, but looks like he don't want any. Mrs. Ping's got the one for that — he wants to all the time. She says it makes her so mad at him, and she's afraid he wouldn't talk after that, but the lady who sells them says it don't make any difference, might make him talk more! Like braggin'!"

It was the ringing of the telephone that shut Mom off. I turned away from her and just then Uncle Parley Dooks came shuffling in from the kitchen. Uncle Parley was a weazened little pensioner of the railroad company. He took tottering little steps, couldn't see good, and was so humped that he was a foot shorter than his wife, my acidulous Aunt Maud. He had been a fire builder for the Burlington Route away back when men crawled inside the fireboxes of locomotives and started fires with kindling and waste soaked in signal oil.

"Hello, Uncle Parley," I said. "How'd you get over here?"

He lived only a few blocks away, but liked to be codded about his shuffling walk and how long it took him to get from where he was to some place else. "Hello, Boley. Oh, Millie wanted to come, so I and Maud though if we could get Manford to bring us we'd come over for a few minutes. So I went to the telephone and the first time I got my finger in the wrong holes and —"

"Shut up!" Aunt Maud snapped.

Aunt Maud is skinny as a hatpin and has a knot on her neck. She always looked as though she had just swallowed a dose of quinine, and her temperament matched her expression.

"Hello, Aunt Maud," I said. "Too bad about Aunt Prue, wasn't it?"

"Have you found out about the will? How much money did she leave?"

"I don't think she left much," I storied. "Don't know yet."

"She left more than you think, thataway and that," Aunt Maud said mysteriously, and glanced apprehensively at her sister Millie.

My Aunt Millie is a spinster, and she lives with Aunt Maud and Uncle Parley. She had been sitting on the couch, and now she got up and waved her arms, which was a sign that she was going to mumble something.

Aunt Millie has a thin red face, and when she tries

to talk she sounds a great deal like an excited turkey gobbler. Redden her nose a little more and make it more limber and it would do for a gobbler's dangling tab.

"Oh, my poor little sister! Oh, poor sister Prue that had to die away out there all alone without a man!" I think it was that Aunt Millie gobbled—when Mom later interpreted the jabberwock—and waved her arms.

If you stand a yard or so away from Aunt Millie when she gobbles and waves her arms you aren't in any danger, but look out if you happen to be near her. For she pumps her arms out and up like a weight-lifter doing a jerk-and-press and a snatch at the same time. Aunt Millie's greatest burden, that she was doomed to bear all her life, was her virginity. In her eighties she was still waving her arms and deploring in her half-hysterical gobbler's cry, "I tell you if I had it to do over again I'd get in bed with a man ever' chance I got. They ain't nothin' like havin' a man in your bed, thataway and that!"

There were quite a few people who considered Millie Dinnegan "lackin'," as they say down in my old home country of Spunky Ridge, ever since her childhood, when she went with Aunt Prue one day to saw into a bee tree and get the honey. They took head-nets, bee smoker, ax, saw, rope and half a barrel that had been sawed off just above its bungholes. Tying one end of the rope in the bungholes, they looped the other end over a limb, and Aunt Prue climbed overhand, while Aunt Millie stood in the half barrel to balance Aunt Prue's weight on the other end of the rope. Aunt Prue smoked the bee hole good, widened it with the ax and saw, and started loading honey into the wooden tub that Aunt Millie had pulleyed up. Aunt Millie didn't weigh much, and it wasn't long till she felt herself being lifted; but she held on even when the tub banged her head and knocked off her head-net as it shot down. She bumped her head again on the limb, of course, and when the tub hit the ground it came apart, and thus relieved of its honey, its two staves with the bungholes in them shot back up and cracked Aunt Millie's head again as *she* came down. Aunt Millie hit the ground like a sack of bran, let go the rope, she was so stunned, and the pieces of barrel with the bungholes in them of course dropped on her head. Aunt Prue once described the incident to me. "It was a vivid demonstration," she said, "of the laws of gravitation."

Mom always told, "It all happened so fast, five bangs in one, you might say, that Millie took on her head, thataway and that, all the bee stingers, too, that it was no wonder Millie was lackin' afterwards. She was so swole up when she got home that when I went to give her a drink of water I got it in her ear—couldn't tell where her mouth or anything else was at."

The only thing wrong with generous Mom's explanation of Aunt Millie's odd behavior, according to my Uncle LankyFrank Dinnegan, was that Millie was just as lackin' before the bee-tree business as she was afterward.

Finished for the time being with the telephone, Mom asked me, "Did you hear anything more from that lawyer or Mr. Tootle?"

"No. I just got in the car and came down as soon as the train got in. Rembrandt said there weren't any telegrams or phone calls at the house."

"Ain't this been a kind of a sad day, Rembrandt?" Mom said. She is plump and white-haired, and comes only to Brandy's shoulders. Whenever I see my mother and my wife together, the one old and gray and the other getting that way, I'm thankful that I was born of one and married to the other. They crossed the room and sat down next to Aunt Millie on the couch.

"It certainly was a surprise to us," Rembrandt said. "When the phone rang we just thought maybe something had happened to The Folly again and Boley wouldn't have to work today, but could go fishing." And away they went on the job of bringing each other uptodate on women's talk.

Cousin Manford and I got out in the kitchen by ourselves where we could talk without the women interfering. "I see Mom's got a funeral wreath on the door knob," I said. "Wonder what else has been done."

"Nothing much, I guess," Manford said. "I didn't know anything about it till I got home from work tonight. I guess everybody in town knew it before I did, the way Mom and Aunt Molly used the phone."

Cousin Manford Dooks owned a cold-storage business in Saganois and rented out food lockers. He was about my age, a big, raw-boned hillbilly with freckles and bushy red hair.

"Did you call Uncle LankyFrank?"

"Mom called him. He'll be up tomorrow. I guess they want to wait on LankyFrank and Bonnie and anybody else that wants to come before they make any definite funeral arrangements."

"I called Gib Parker at the funeral home today noon. He's expecting Aunt Prue Friday afternoon on No. 57 from St. Louis. I thought if we could get things ready and have the funeral Friday afternoon, we could get all done before dark, if the sermon wasn't too long. Wonder what church they'll decide on. What was Aunt Prue, anyway?"

Cousin Manford sort of let out his breath in little giggling jerks and reached for his cigarettes. "She wasn't much of anything, was she? She maintained that she always went to the church closest to where she happened to be on Sundays."

"Mom's a Baptist, I guess. What's Aunt Maud?"

"Mom's a Methodist, or supposed to be, but she don't work much at it."

"They'll have to fight that out between themselves, what preacher to have."

"They'll fight, all right."

"How is your mother feeling these days?"

"All right. Poisonous as ever. Mad all the time. To hear her tell it, I and Edith didn't raise our kids right and our kids ain't raisin' their kids right. I don't see how Dad stands her. The other day she wanted me to drop everything and come over and spade her garden. When I told her she was eighty-three years old and didn't need a garden, damned if she didn't get out and spade it herself. I hired a man to do it but she run the guy out of the yard with her spade."

"She's old, Manny, and you have to overlook a lot of things that people do when they get old."

"Oh, she's been that way all her life. Remember when she and your mother were over in Spunky Ridge taking care of Grandma Dinnegan just before she died, and Mom said that if she ever got as mean and cranky as Grandma Dinnegan was before she died, she hoped somebody would hit her in the head with an ax?"

I nodded. "Mom told me."

"I told Edith the other day, after Mom spaded her own garden, that it was about time to start swingin'."

"Whatever they decide about the church or the preacher is all right with me. The main thing is to get Aunt Prue planted as soon as we can. By Friday she'll be dead five days anyway."

"I could put her in my zero room and freeze her solid, but we don't want to do that unless we have to. They do it, though, sometimes, when the grave-digger's union calls a strike. Out in Oakland, California a few years ago they had corpses in cold storage all over town."

"Yeah, I remember reading about it, but I hope we don't have to do that. I guess she should be buried alongside Uncle Phin in that three-cornered cemetery on top of Snake Mountain, where Grandpa and Grandma Dinnegan sit in their chairs. Or are they still there?"

Living in Saganois, on the edge of the Spunky Ridge country, Manford had kept more abreast with the doings down there than I had. He still hunted quails and stuff down there, which was the old home country of both of us.

"Oh, yes, they're still there—they'll still be sitting there a thousand years from now unless an atomic bomb hits close. I shot two quail last fall damn' near off old Grandpa Dinnegan's nose."

"I killed a fox one time in that red-top grass when I was hunting rabbits. He came trotting up over the hill and when he saw me he turned and high-tailed it right down the fence past the concrete statues. I let him have it right in the caboose. That old Dinnegan cemetery is a good hunting spot. Devil of a place to get to, though. Those old-timers wouldn't think of burying anybody on ground that was level enough to farm."

The Dinnegan cemetery was a three-cornered patch of about four acres, with an iron fence built around it. Old Grandpa Dinnegan had built forms and poured his and Grandma's monuments in concrete long before he died. The old man had done a good job in creating likenesses of himself and his wife. Grandpa was a straight-backed, fierce-looking man in a long-tailed coat, and Grandma wore Dolly Varden clothes—except the hat, the long feathers of which Grandpa couldn't reproduce in concrete, so he left his wife bareheaded—and her hair was bound smooth and tight against her head. Aunt Prue told me once that Grandpa Dinnegan was a man of great personal pride and would have preferred to make himself a concrete plug hat, or at least a cady, to cover his baldness, but the Dolly Varden plumes of the day stumped him, so he sacrificed his dignity for grandma and went to Heaven bareheaded, the same as she did.

The statues sat in one corner of the triangular cemetery. It was Grandfather Dinnegan's plan that his children, grandchildren, great grandchildren and so on would all be buried in his cemetery, and thus their graves would fan out, one generation after the other, behind him and grandma, who started it all.

Cousin Mansford and I got to talking about hunting and fishing, and we stayed so long out in the kitchen that Aunt Maud sent Uncle Parley out to get us. He came tottering through the kitchen door and mumbled, "Maud wants you to come in the other room so ever'body can talk things over."

"Tell her to come out here," Manford said.

"I can't go back and tell Maud that," Uncle Parley said. "You know how she is, thataway and that. She'd put a tin ear on me. You better holler in there yourself or else—"

"Shut up!" Aunt Maud said from the doorway. She came stalking in on her thin stilt legs—"Six ax handles to the first knothole," Aunt Prue used to say of her—with Mom and Rembrandt an Aunt Millie following her.

"If you won't come in there I'll come out here," Aunt Maud said beligerently. "I got something to tell you that I been savin' up ever since I talked to Bonnie this morning."

"What's the matter, Mom?" Manford said. "Out of Parena?"

"No, I ain't out of Parena. But I bet I know something that you fellers don't," Aunt Maud said ominously.

"About sister Prue."

Aunt Maud and her addiction to the patent medicine called Parena was quite a family joke. She required a shot of it several times a day, she said, for her nerves. I was the culprit who discovered Aunt Maud's secret. I was down at Saganois hunting ducks one season years ago and ran out of ammunition. When I started downtown to get more shotgun shells one night after supper, Aunt Maud asked me to get her a bottle of Parena. I did, and when I happened to glance at the label on the bottle saw that it was marked 80 percent alcohol. The concoction contained only enough other ingredients to kill the whisky odor. And ever since, in Aun Maud's baleful eyes, I've been a scoundrel, a rascal and a general bad man. Because although Aunt Maud would stay up till midnight playing Rook and drinking Parena, she would never dream of playing pinochle and drinking beer, and occasionally I codded her about it.

"What do you know about Aunt Prue — Aunt Maud?"

"I bet you didn't know she had a fifty-thousand-dollar life-insurance policy!" Aunt Maud snapped.

"Fifty thousand dollars!" I said. "Gee whiz!"

"I should say so, gee whiz," Uncle Parley said.

"Shut up!" Aunt Maud said. "She took it out with Charles' company in 1929. Bonnie told me today over the phone. We'll know more about it when she gets down here tomorrow night."

Charles, Cousin Bonnie's husband, was Mr. Charles Willard Stabbs. He worked for the Great Lakes Mutual Life Insurance Company of Chicago. Used words like jest and acquiesce and longevity.

I saw that the news stunned Manford. He had told me a few minutes before how badly he needed a new compressor for his deep freeze. I knew he was thinking about his chances of inheriting some of Aunt Prue's insurance money.

"No, I guess Charles didn't know anything about it himself," Aunt Maud said, "even if he does work for the company, it happened so long ago, before he started working there. The way Bonnie talked, he didn't know anything about it till this lawyer Mr. Stambo called the insurance company early this morning."

"Is Charles working in the office now or is he still collecting from door to door?" I asked. I didn't trust my cousin Bonnie's husband any farther than I could spit against the wind.

"Oh, he's been in the office quite a while now. He works where they handle the wills."

"I need a new roof on my house," Mom said. She was too stunned by the news to talk any more just then about kindred subjects of roofs and houses.

"Why, Mom," I said, "you wouldn't want any of Aunt Prue's money, would you?"

"Well, if she's got that much I ort to come in for my part. I don't want to be like my second cousin Lyman's third wife, Allie May, Lyman only left the little fixin' a dollar, and her the mother of all them wood's colts, she had to use the law to get her part."

Mom was going to tell more about Lyman's third wife, but Aunt Millie, back by the door, began to pump her arms and make noises.

"If I had a lot of money, and I died, and had a poor old sister that didn't have no man to take care of her, I would leave her some money," Aunt Millie gobbled. "I wouldn't be content to let her spend her last days livin' with another sister, thataway and that."

It was almost ten oclock before we got through talking about the insurance policy. Cousin Manford finally said, "I guess we all better get to bed and wait till tomorrow when Bonnie comes down and we know more about it."

"I'm going to tell Mrs. Plink," Mom said, and started for the telephone. "She took care of Prudence once when she was ailing with the shingles, maybe Prue will leave her a little something, Lottie Plink is poorly and it might make her feel better."

"Oh, Mom, not now," I said. "Wait till morning."

But Mom called Mrs. Plink, a sprightly widow who lived next door, anyway.

As we were getting ready for bed I said to Rembrandt, "Quite a surprise, huh, that insurance policy?"

"Nothing that your Aunt Prue did would surprise me. Didn't I tell you she was something of a witch? She was Pollyanna, the glad girl. I think her spirit is laughing at us right now."

"Wonder who will get the Cadillac?"

"Now, Boley."

"Always wanted a Cadillac. Lots of power. Big trunk. I could even haul a moose home from Canada in it."

6 Mom and Rembrandt and I were still sitting at the breakfast table Wednesday morning when my Uncle LankyFrank Dinnegan and his wife Aunt Birdella arrived. Their battered old Chevvy was speckled with dried-up, yellow Spunky Ridge mud, for they lived in the middle of the hilliest section, not more than four or five miles from Snake Mountain, which sits exactly on top of the main hogback.

Uncle LankyFrank walks in surges, a habit acquired from tramping hills. He even pumps his body backwards and forwards when he is driving his car up-hill, as though by so doing he might help it negotiate the steep ascents. For Spunky Ridge has hills so pointed that cars need creeper gears going over them, higher drive shafts to keep from grazing their crests, and special radiator caps to hold the water in when going down them — if a slight and traditional hillbilly exaggeration is permitted.

Mom kissed Uncle LankyFrank and Aunt Birdie, and shed a tear or two, then led them into the kitchen. LankyFrank wore a brand new pair of bib overalls and a black felt hat, and Aunt Birdella had on a black coat and a fascinator tied around her head.

"Hello, Boley," LankyFrank said. "I ain't seen you for a — century."

"How are you, Frank? Aunt Birdie." I shook hands

with both of them. One thing about a Spunky Ridge funeral: You meet a lot of relation you haven't seen for a long time.

Of all my hillbilly relatives, Uncle LankyFrank is my favorite. He is tall and skinny, limber as a hickory switch, and just as tough. At seventy-five his hair is still black and thick and curly. He has a thin, dark, sardonic face, and lively black eyes. I have never known LankyFrank to be solemn about anything, even funerals:

"Prue died, huh?"

"Yes," Mom said, "she passed away. I can't hardly believe it. Left fifty thousand dollars, too, and maybe a good deal more, with the car and her houses and all."

"She did!"

"That's what Maud told us last night that Bonnie told her over the phone yesterday."

"She'll sure have a big funeral then. Ever'body will think if they come to the funeral they might get something. That's what she told around."

"Aw," Mom said. "She didn't either. You just made that up. I know you."

"That's what she told Bascom Twog down at the Left Hand Hill Store," Aunt Birdie said. "I heared her. But then they was always a-coddlin' each other, thataway and that."

Aunt Birdie is a comfortable, grandmotherly little person and she likes to tell a story:

"No, Prue was going to buy a dressed chicken from Bascom—Guldy-Pete Rye had killed off all his chickens when his woman got so bad with the female trouble that she couldn't see after them, and sold them to Bascom. And when Prue was in the store lookin' at 'em she picked up one. Then she told Bascom that it smelt like it was a little swizzly. They got to jowing about one thing and another, and finally Prue bet him she'd outlive him even if he was twenty-five years younger than he was, and if she lost the bet for him to show up at her funeral and she'd pay it.

So they bet ten dollars. That's the way all the talk got started, I guess. We seen Matt Hicks at the ferry on our way up here and he said he sure would go to the funeral if he as going to get paid ten dollars for doing it."

Even Rembrandt was laughing at Aunt Birdella, and Mom said, "I never knowed about that, but I wouldn't put it past her." She was disappointed not to have heard the story before, so that she could properly edit and embellish it for presentation to her listening public. "Did she take the chicken?"

"Sure she did. There wasn't anything the matter with it. Bascom sure carried her high about it. It's a wonder you never heard about it, the way Bascom told it around."

I guess we would have sat there talking all day, but the telephone rang, Belshazzar cackled "Somebody-at-the-door," and the call was from Aunt Maud. She and the rest of them were down at the funeral home waiting for us to meet them there and make arrangements. We could hear her clear out in the kitchen:

"Is Frank and Birdella there yet?"

"Yes, they're here," Mom said. "We been talkin'."

"Well, ye bettern come on down right away. We ain't got all day. It's nine oclock already."

"Parley's prob'ly faunchin'," Uncle LankyFrank snickered.

"Pretty soon we'll hear her tell him to shut up," I predicted, "and he 'better run' then."

The thought of poor old Uncle Parley Dooks doing any faunchin' around Aunt Maud tickled Rembrandt, who was still laughing about Aunt Prue and the swizzly chicken. "You should be ashamed of yourselves," Rem scolded. "Aunt Maud means well."

Just then we heard Aunt Maud yell SHUT UP, and Brandy for once lost her dignity and howled.

"We'll be down right away," Mom told Aunt Maud. She hung up and came back to the kitchen. "My, but she's mad. They been waitin' down there since eight oclock. I been thinkin': I bet it was in 1922, and I was busy with the railroad strike that I didn't hear about Prue and the chicken."

Gib Parker's funeral home was the only one in Saganois. The town isn't big enough for an undertaker to make a living in it by just burying people, so Gib ran a furniture and household appliance business in his store except on days he had funerals. Then he just carried the davenports, chairs, tables and other stuff out of the display room, set up his portable pulpit, unfolded a few wooden chairs, called his store a chapel and held the funeral.

When we got down there the furniture was still in the main room, but Gib had set up the pulpit and was leaning on it. He was a skinny, middle-aged man, and wore a black suit and a collar that was too big. He greeted us and arranged us around the room, setting us on whatever was handy.

"I guess we're all here," Aunt Maud announced acidly. "Finally." She glared at LankyFrank, who scowled back at her. "Guess we can go ahead now."

Mr. Parker cleared his throat:

"On this sad occasion, as we gather to decide those matters that are necessary following the death of a loved one, I first of all wish to express my deepest sympathy for you in this, your hour of sorrow. As you know, Mrs. Persnosky passed away far from home — more than two thousand miles from home. That is regrettable, of course, but cannot be helped. I am sure that Mr. Wang, the undertaker who prepared the body for burial, has done all within his power and skill to insure its arrival here promptly and in a condition conducive to a proper and dignified funeral. He has sent word that the body will be here day after tomorrow – Friday – on the afternoon train from St. Louis.

"Under the unusual circumstances of Mrs. Persnosky's death, my duties as the undertaker are of an extremely minor nature, compared to what they normally would have been. However, that does not detract from my desire to help you folks in any way I can; and you are most welcome to use my grass, hearse, tent, flower racks or any other equipment that I have."

Mr. Parker talked so nice and kind that Aunt Maud simmered down, and even was a bit abashed. She had written a list of things to be done on a sheet of tablet paper, and kept waving it significantly all through the first part of Mr. Parker's talk, but by the time he finished, Aunt Maud's paper was barely moving.

"I suggest," Mr. Parker continued, "that we make our tentative arrangements in chronological order, beginning with the arrival of the body at 1:33 Friday afternoon. Do you wish services held in church or here in the chapel? Or would you prefer that all the services be conducted at the cemetery? There is, of course, the matter of time to be considered – the train may be late."

"Why not a short service at the Methodist Church, and then go out to the cemetery and have the main one, thataway and that?" Aunt Maud said.

"Or else the Baptist Church," Mom said. "Reverend Gordon knew sister Prue all his life – him and her was always rafflin'."

"Reverend Hodges raffled with her, too, don't forget," Aunt Maud said. "At Fish Frys and City Picnics they done awful good on sheets and blankets."

Mr. Parker, astute man, spiked the argumentative

guns that were being unlimbered by saying authoritatively, "That can be settled later. I must mention again, however, the element of time. I have another funeral at two oclock Friday afternoon, over in the Puckerbrush neighborhood, just this side of Shake-Rag schoolhouse."

"Yeah," Frank said. "Boker Trent. I heared he died."

When Mr. Parker mentioned Shake-Rag schoolhouse I saw Aunt Maud crack a smile—not much: Only from her false teeth out—but as much of a smile as the crusty old hatpin ever permitted. All the Dinnegans had gone to school at Shake-Rag, and my Mom and Aunt Prue were responsible for its odd name. The schoolhouse had been built in the 1880's, when the sisters were in their early teens, and already known as brats.

The Sunday night before school started in the new stone building, Mom and Aunt Prue managed to raise a window, climb in and steal the teacher's hand-bell and hang it on a string in the well at one corner of the schoolyard. Next morning when the teacher—Nettie Maloney, it was—wanted to take up school she couldn't find the bell to ring out the front door and thus notify all the kids playing Blackman and Andy Over that it was time for school to take up. She looked everywhere, but no bell. So she just waved an old dust-rag out the door and yelled. Every youngster in the school was soundly paddled by Nettie Maloney, but nobody except the two girls knew anything about the bell, and they wouldn't tell.

Not until years later did they confess the mischief. The string holding the bell rotted and let it fall in the water, where it stayed until around 1900 when Tom Larkey found it while he was installing a new pump. Although the schoolhouse was known as Puckerbrush while it was being built, it was Shake-Rag from its first day of school, and still is.

"I'm not sure that the hearse will have time to service Mr. Trent's funeral and yours, too, expecially if you decide to have the sermon preached in church," Mr. Parker said. "It would be three oclock at least before the hearse could return here, and by the time the body was taken from the depot to the church, and after the sermon, from the church to the cemetery it would be almost dark. I have enough carpet grass and flower racks, and I have another interring elevator, but I have only the one hearse."

"We don't want it to get dark on us at the funeral," Mom said. "That's a bad sign."

I noticed that Aunt Maud still wore her faint reminiscent smile, so I thought it safe to suggest, "We could save time if we sent the casket up to Spunky Ridge on The Folly. That way, the hearse could cut across from Shake-Rag to Spunky Ridge flag stop over the Wildcat Road and meet us there. Of course, all the services would have to be held at the graveyard."

Aunt Maud didn't flare up, but Aunt Millie's arms began to pump. "I've lived eighty-four years," she gobbled gloomily, as near as I could make out her noises, "and I never heared of such a thing!"

"Neither did I," Uncle Parley agreed with her.

"Shut up!" Aunt Maud said.

"Now you, Boley," Aunt Millie said, nodding her thin, gobbler-like head at me, "you ort to know — you got a government job — did you ever hear of such a thing: having all the funeral services outdoors?"

"Remember how Aunt Prue liked the outdoors? Remember when she took Uncle Phin out snipe hunting at night. Gave him a gunnysack and set him on a sandbar in Rocky Branch and told him to hold the sack open while she rounded up the snipes with her bull's-eye lantern and herded them into the sack. She let him shiver an hour or so, then came back and told him there weren't any snipes out that night, and if they wanted anything like snipes to eat they would have to steal a chicken. She had fixed it up with Guldy-Pete Rye to steal one of his Plymouth Rock chickens, which roosted in the trees in Guldy-Pete's front yard. So they doused the lantern and sneaked up into the yard, and while Aunt Prue kept a sharp lookout Uncle Phin climbed up in a tree to steal a chicken. She told Phin to be sure and grab it around the neck so it wouldn't squawk and wake Guldy. So Uncle Phin did, and when he was easing himself back down the tree Aunt Prue yelled as loud as she could, 'Be sure and get a big one!'"

"Yeah," Uncle LankyFrank snickered, "Guldy said Phin took off all the limbs comin' down."

That started it. We got to telling stories about Aunt Prue till even Mom stopped worrying about the weather, the grave caving in, the hearse breaking down, and even the choice of preachers, and enjoyed the fun.

Aunt Maud told about one time when Aunt Prue went to renew her driver's license. She knew she couldn't see well enough to read the letters and figures without her glasses, and as she had forgot to bring her glasses she told the examiner she was so nervous that she had to walk around the room a few times before she took the test. So she kept sashaying past the blackboard and glancing sideways at the letters and figures until she had completely memorized them, knowing the examiner would notice everything about her except where her eyes were looking. "Bonnie can tell about it better than I can," Aunt Maud said, rubbing at the knot on her neck. "She's a writer, you know."

We told so many stories about fabulous Aunt Prue that they finally smothered Aunt Millie's protests against holding all the services at the graveside. Aunt

Prue would travel from Saganois up to Spunky Ridge flag stop in The Folly's baggage car; and the hearse, cutting cross country from Shake-Rag, over the Wildcat Road, would meet the train there and haul the corpse on up to the Dinnegan cemetery on top of Snake Mountain. The main-line train from St. Louis made a close connection with The Folly at Saganois, and if it was on time everything would work out very well. Because it wouldn't take long to transfer Aunt Prue from one train to the other, and we would have everything overwith long before dark.

"If that train ain't on time," worried Mom, "what then?"

"We'll just have to wait," I said. "We can't bury her till she gets here, that's a cinch."

"Have any of you made arrangements for the grave?" Mr. Parker asked.

"Yeah," Uncle LankyFrank said. "The Barnes boys are digging it today. I went over this morning and showed them where to dig. Took a tent along too—I figured you might have yours over at the Puckerbrush funeral."

The Barnes boys, Lafe and Wally, were in their sixties at least, but to Frank they would always be boys. I guess it was because the skinny brothers never married. They had dug all the graves in the Dinnegan cemetery that had been dug in the last forty years.

"They was going to dig out a couple of fox dens while they're at it," Frank said.

"Thank you for the use of the tent," Mr. Parker said. "I guess that about completes the arrangements, except the choice of a minister."

"I say Reverend Gordon," Mom said, doubling up her argumentive fists."

"Reverend Hodges," Aunt Maud said, bringing up her guard.

Just then in walked Latrum Squall, the colored boy who worked for Saganois Post Master, John Poole, with a Special Delivery Air Mail letter. I noticed the postmark first thing: Pistol River, Oregon, and I knew it was from Mr. Stambo, Mr. Chin or Mr. Tootle, the man who ran the motel out there and who spelled his name T-c-z-e-t-l.

Latrum Squall trundled the mail cart to and from the depot, janitored the Post Office, and in his spare time barbered colored folks in the rearmost chair of Mr. Poole's barber shop next door, in the same building.

"This just come on The Folly," Latrum said importantly, "and I left a customer in the chair to bring it over right away. Hello, Mr. Paydoley."

I nodded, realizing suddenly that we had spent all morning with Mr. Parker. "Guess my sub cleaned up all the mail coming down."

"A good substitute, that Mr. Scott," Latrum said gravely. "Always ties the Special Delivery letters on top of the packages so they will be noticed right away. That way, no time is lost in delivering them." The Saganois Post Office averaged receiving about two special deliveries a week, but that did not prevent the grave responsibility of handling the United States rails from resting heavily on Latrum's conscience.

The combination Post Office and barber shop was right across the street from the funeral home, and Mr. Squall didn't have far to go to earn his few extra cents by delivering the important piece of mail. He still wore his white barber's jacket, and a straight-edge razor was stuck above one ear.

The letter was from Mr. Stambo. Mr. Parker read it aloud to all of us, including Latrum, who waited expectantly:

"Dear Mr. Parker:

"Enclosed is a note found in Mrs. Persnosky's effects—all of which have not repeat not been examined yet, incidentally—which is of interest to you and to Mrs. Persnosky's relatives. It is mailed to you by the fastest possible means in the hope that it reaches you in time for you to comply with its extremely unusual requests regarding the last rites of the deceased.
> Yours,
> John Stambo, Atty.,
> Pistol River, Oregon."

Aunt Prue's note was headed Instructions To Director Of My Funeral. Mr. Parker read:

"I want to be planted beside my husband, Phineas Persnosky, in the Dinnegan cemetery on top of Snake Mountain near Spunky Ridge (P.O. Vinton) Starbuck County, Illinois. It is immaterial to me what denominational service is held as long as it is conducted by the Reverend Alvin Hoosh, of Limberswitch, in the Spunky Ridge hills. Especially if Pastor Hoosh still has his longhorn mustache. If Alvin is unable to conduct the service by himself, or at least a part of it, I want his daughter, Mrs. Carrie Papp, to help him.

"I also want Mrs. Bonnie Dooks Stabbs' story *Lost Moments* read at the graveside. Probably the shortest version of it would be the most appropriate. I want the service to include the singing of the hymn *Shall We Gather At The River*, and rendition of the ditty *Turkey In The Straw*—on the zither. I have no other requests to make except that everyone have fun.
> Signed:
> Mrs. Prudence Persnosky.

"P.S.: Note to Boley Paydoley: Pay Bascom Twog ten dollars—I wagered that I would outlive him—unless he's dead, of course. P.P."

7 Aunt Prue had played many unorthodox tricks on us during her long life, but never anything as bizarre as this. We all sat like turtles on a log for quite a few seconds. The only move I saw anybody make since early in the reading of the instructions was when Rembrandt edged closer to me on the davenport, found my hand, and I could feel her body shiver. I remembered what she had said about Aunt Prue being a witch.

Latrum Squall was still standing near the pulpit when Mr. Parker finished reading. His mouth was hanging open and his eyes had popped and were rolling alarmingly. As soon as he had recovered sufficiently to move he tore back across the street to his waiting, lathered customer, his white coat tails flat with speed.

"Well," Mom said finally, and drew a long breath, "that's that, thataway and that."

"About the preacher, you mean," Aunt Maud said. "Al Hoosh. He ain't preached since he was at Little Buck church. I and Parley was married at Little Buck." She looked actually tender at Uncle Parley and smiled a gentle reminiscence, more than just from the teeth out.

Emboldened by the smile, Uncle Parley said, "He married Manford and Edith here in Saganois, too. He was out in the field cuttin' shock corn with a corn knife, but he dropped ever'thing to marry them. That was in 1917, and Manford was gettin' ready to go to the army and didn't have much time. Edith was a big strong woman and—" Uncle Parley broke off into a mumble as he saw Aunt Maud getting ready to yell SHUT UP at him.

Aunt Millie waved her arms a time or two, but the funeral instructions had left her noiseless. In fact, it was two days before she recovered sufficiently to make any sounds at all. Mom was worried that she had been stricken dumb.

"Who is this Reverend Hoosh?" I asked Uncle Frank.

"Lives over in the Limberswitch country. George Papp married his daughter Carrie. Farms some. Hunts and traps." Uncle LankyFrank's black eyes grew animated as he paid Mr. Hoosh the highest compliment one hillbilly can pay another:

"Got some good foxhounds!"

"How old is he?"

"About my age—we went to school together."

"Humph!" Mom snorted, "he was a mean one, he was. He was going to throw Frank in the Shake-Rag privy hole head first, one time, and had him halfway in when I got there. So I just pulled Frank out and stuck Alvin in himself—feet first. I was in the girls's privy when I heard him yell."

It must be mentioned here that in Mom's day, down in my old home country of Spunky Ridge, kids went to grade school till they got married.

"Al's seventy-four, Aunt Pop told me the other day," Aunt Birdella said. "I saw her up at Vinton."

"Aunt Pop?" I asked.

"That's George Papp's wife Carrie, the one Aunt Prue meant. She's a preacher, too."

"Aunt Pop Papp?"

"Sounds like a double-barrel shotgun, don't it?" Uncle LankyFrank said.

"How come they call her Aunt Pop?"

"I don't know. They just do."

"Well, it was Bascom Twog called her that first, down at the Left Hand Hill Store," Mom spoke up. "He told around that she got to talkin' so fast that she started poppin'."

"You say she's a preacher, too?"

"Oh, yes," Aunt Birdella said. "She preaches at Little Buck church ever' once in a while. Gives poems and readings, too; and they're different in the way they sound when they're *given* instead of just reading them. What was that one, Frank, that tickled us so much — *Pigs Is Pigs*, that's it. We both laughed fit to kill."

Aunt Birdella went on to relate the highlights of Mr. Ellis Parker Butler's well-known yarn about the baggage-master and the crate of guinea pigs, and when she had finished it was plain that she looked forward with pleasure to hearing Aunt Pop Papp *give Lost Moments* at the funeral.

"She'll have to do most of the preachin'," Uncle LankyFrank said. "Al's got the asmy so bad he can't talk very long at a time. Get's to wheezin'."

"Wheezing, huh," I said. "Does Reverned Hoosh still have a mustache?"

"I *maintain* he's got a mustache!" Uncle LankyFrank said. "About a foot long. Hangs down six inches on each side."

"Oh, it ain't quite that long, Frank," Aunt Maud said. "But it does hang down quite a ways."

I was beginning to get the drift of Aunt Prue's diabolical strategy. With Reverend Hoosh's long mustache waving in his wheezes, and Aunt Pop Papp *giving Lost Moments*, not to mention *Turkey In The Straw* on the zither, Aunt Prue had done all she could to provide fun and entertainment for everyone attending her funeral – which was exactly what she could be expected to do.

"I guess we'll have to drive over and see Al and Aunt Pop," Uncle LankyFrank said, "and make arrangements with them."

"Can't we call them on the phone?" I asked.

"No," Aunt Birdella said, "he don't have no phone. He was going to run a line down through the brush on a bobwire fence to his place – started it but never finished it. Said he just got tired cuttin' brush."

I knew how it was – we live on a brush-and-gully place ourselves. A good part of the Spunky Ridge telephone lines used standing trees for poles, and every year the ever-growing brush and foliage had to be cleared away from them. "We can look him up this afternoon," I said.

"You all come out to my house for dinner," Mom said. "I got ham and chicken and some other grub ready."

Mom and her sisters would have liked to ride down through their old home country, but didn't feel quite up to making the trip. The excitement of making the funeral arrangements according to Aunt Prue's instructions was just too exhausting.

"Besides," Mom said, "I got to warsh out a few pieces;" and Aunt Maud and Uncle Parley had to go with Manford and Edith to meet Cousin Bonnie when she came in on the train from Chicago. As for Aunt Millie, she went straight to bed as soon as she ate lunch, she was so horror-stricken.

So Uncle LankyFrank and I started out to find the Reverend Alvin Hoosh and his daughter, Aunt Pop Papp. "I'll take my car," I suggested.

LankyFrank codded me, "Got a radiator cap on it that don't leak?"

"Just an ordinary cap."

"Better take my car. We have to go up and down Andy Over pinnacle."

Andy Over wasn't as high as Snake Mountain but it was steeper. I went along with what Mr. Charles Willard Stabbs, Cousin Bonnie's husband, would call the jest. "O.K.," I said.

Uncle LankyFrank had an old Chevvy sedan with a four-speed truck transmission in it, and thus had a creeper "grandma" gear he could use on the worst hills, some of which, according to Spunky Ridge tradition were straight up and down and even hung over a little.

We crossed Saganois River and headed northwest, in past Tom Larkey's place, on a fairly good graveled road until we hit the Wildcat Road. Then down past the Left Hand Hill Store and the burned ruins of the Right Hand Hill Store across the road from it, along the swampy edge of Turtle Holler, and on to climb Andy Over—steep as a house roof—and toward Puckerbrush. I had Frank stop on top of Andy so I could look under the car and see how much clearance the drive shaft had going over the prong, and there was little enough to sponsor the hillbilly gag. In fact it was so steep that we could start rivulets in opposite directions just by swinging a few degrees this way or that.

The Spunky Ridge country is part of the fag end of the Ozarks. God must have been in a whimsical mood when He took a handful of hills from the west side of the Mississippi River and flung them across into Illinois—and let none of the beauty of the Ozark vales and hollows, prongs and pinnacles, and rocks and rills dribble through His fingers when He made the toss.

On this bright April afternoon the grass had begun to green in the warm sun, and the buds of trees to appear — almost as big as a squirrel's foot, the maple buds were, and high time to plant corn. Morel mushrooms, gray and brown cone-shaped sponges, sprouted on every sun-baked hillside, and Jack-In-The-Pulpits, Dutchman's Britches, Johnny Jump-ups and fragile blue violets peeped from the clumps of May Apples that were to be found in every wooded dell. The voice of the turtle was pleasing to the eye.

This was my beloved old home country, the place where I was born: Spunky Ridge, a fragment of the United States, the memories of which was my heritage:

Shake-Rag schoolhouse where kids began their day by bowing their heads and reciting The Lord's Prayer, then stood to pledge allegiance to Old Glory, and sing *My Country, 'Tis Of Thee* or *Columbia, The Gem Of The Ocean* or some other proud and patriotic song; Little Buck church where people humbled themselves in a careful, old-time religion; Left Hand Hill Store where statesmen were elected; Dinnegan cemetery where my ancestors slept.

This was the section of America that I knew best — though I hadn't spent much time there in recent years, more's the pity. To preserve its way of life I had twice donned a military uniform. I didn't want its freedom challenged or even threatened. I had lived too many years as a free American to ever want to live any other way. I would much rather die.

The Reverend Alvin Hoosh lived with his daughter Carrie and her husband, farmer-hunter-trapper George Papp. Their house sat on a hillside, and its front porch was level with the shoulder of the road when Uncle LankyFrank drove up in front of it and stopped. Three beautiful white-and-tan Walker fox hounds roused from their naps in various parts of the sloping side-yard and greeted us with much tail-wagging and a chorus of friendly barks. "Get ready for the speakin'," Frank warned me.

We heard Aunt Pop before we saw her: "Mr. Dinnegan, I declare! I heard that Prue had passed away, and I have been praying for her and thinking of you and Molly and Millie and Maud and their families, it is indeed unfortunate that she passed away all alone away out there but it was the will of the Lord and who are we to doubt the wisdom of His ways, won't you come in?"

Aunt Pop was well nicknamed. She came talking through the front door, a middle-aged, vital, black-eyed woman with a steeply shelving bosom and wide across the pockets. Mr. Hoosh was behind her, and we saw his mustache before we saw him. He had drawn the shades to shut out the bright sun while he took his afternoon nap on the couch in the front room, and in the gloom his white drooping muctachio waved eerily as he followed his daughter out onto the porch.

"Hello, Carrie," Uncle LankyFrank said. "How are you, Al? This is Mr. Paydoley, my nephew."

"Molly Paydoley's boy!" Mrs. Papp said excitedly. "You're the one who has the government job handling the United States mails, Oh, the glamor and the romance of such a calling tearing through the night across the river and through the woods over hill and dale neither snow nor rain nor cold nor gloom of night shall stay you from your appointed rounds!"

I thought no, except maybe a faulty trickle valve now and then. I finally got a how-do-you-do in edgeways, and so did Reverend Hoosh. The minister was small and withered. His mustache waved a little even when he said howdy and I imagined how it would oscillate if he preached outdoors, especially if there was a slight breeze or he pushed a bit too hard on p's and b's.

"It was too bad about sister Persnosky," Hoosh said.

"When will the funeral be held? Carrie and I both intend to go."

"That's what we come down to see you about, Al," Uncle LankyFrank said.

"My aunt wanted you to conduct the service," I said. "She left instructions to that effect—she left a whole set of explicit instructions."

"Of course," Reverend Hoosh said, "I shall be glad to. I haven't been very active the last few years, but I shall be glad to do what I can. Carrie sometimes helps me out."

"Aunt Prue suggested that."

"Mrs. Persnosky's request is not unexpected." Mrs. Papp had obviously adjusted her carburetor, and now spoke with more dignity and less boom, also slower. "The last time I saw her she mentioned the kind of ceremony she wanted. Papa and I have prepared a service that I think she would like. We speak alternately. It is a beautiful last rite: allegorical, and concerns a bright sun about to set."

"All the services will be held at the cemetery and we hope to be all through before sundown," I said.

"That will be fine—all the better—more significant," Mrs. Papp said. "We will take care of everything."

"She wants you to give a reading," Uncle LankyFrank said timidly.

Mrs. Papp's fleshy face beamed. "I shall be more than glad to do that. Do you know what type of elocution the reading requires? Dramatic, like *Crossing The Bar* or *Oh, Captain, My Captain,* or perhaps sentimental or tender in a religious way?"

"All I know is it is called *Lost Moments,*" Uncle LankyFrank said. "Bonnie—Maud's girl—wrote it. She's been working on it all her life."

"Oh, yes, I understand she is literarily inclined."

"She's writing on the obit now," I said, "and will have it ready for you in time, I think."

"When is the funeral?" Mr. Hoosh wanted to know.

I explained all the details of the arrangements we had made, omitting only *Turkey In The Straw* on the zither, and asked, "You'll be there then?"

"Oh, yes. We'll be there."

"Thank you."

There were a few more polite social remarks, as required by Spunky Ridge etiquette, as well as a hike down across a field to say the expected hello to George Papp, a slow and goopy man, whom we could see burning cornstalks on his bottom land along Rocky Branch, and then Uncle LankyFrank and I headed for home.

On the way I said, "I guess that about takes care of everything except the zither. Where in Sam Hill are we going to find a zither, much less somebody to tinkle one? You hardly ever see one of those things any more. In fact, the only one I ever saw was its picture in the dictionary."

We were going along thinking about where we might find a zither and somebody to pluck its strings when we came to the Left Hand Hill Store. "Let's stop and have a coke," I suggested. "I haven't seen Professor Twog since I was down here hunting quails in 1950. Besides, I might as well pay him his ten dollars now."

"Funny she would want you to do that," Uncle LankyFrank said. "But then nobody ever knowed what Prue would do next. She sure was the pawky one, thataway and that."

"Professor" Bascom Twog and his wife Lizzie owned and operated the Left Hand Hill Store on the bank of Yorkynut Slough where the Wildcat Road drops down from the main hogback of Spunky Ridge. Bascom isn't a real professor, but only looks, talks and acts like one. He was a short, neat, roly-poly man with blooming pink cheeks and a gray goatee, always taking correspondence courses in subjects like Taxidermy, Business Management and Foremanship, which was why he was known as "professor." He was sitting in his homemade hickory armchair, which was tipped back against the open door of his store, when we pulled up and stopped.

"Well, if it isn't Bolander Paydoley," Bascom greeted me, his lively blue eyes peering welcome over the tops of his iron-rimmed spectacles. He let his chair tip forward on its front legs, then stood up. "The only quail hunter I ever saw empty his pumpgun at a crippled bird flying around and around him in a circle, and miss every shot."

"You never forget anything, do you?" I said. "Give us a couple of cokes and have one yourself."

"How are you, Boley? Say, Frank, this calls for more than innocuous Coca Cola—you haven't killed any Spunky Ridge birds in a long time, have you, Boley?"

"No, I haven't."

"Their survival should be appropriately celebrated. I left two barrels of cider out in the orchard last fall. Along in January, bored a hole through the side of them and bottled what didn't freeze. A hundred and forty proof! Want to try some with your cokes?"

We tried some. The stuff was as strong as applejack; in fact, I guess it was real applejack. It had a kick like a 30-06 with a 220-grain bullet. Over the drinks Bascom asked, "What brings you down here this time of year?"

"Aunt Prue died. We came down to see Al Hoosh about preaching the funeral."

"Prudence Persnosky dead!" The cheerful face saddened. "I'm sorry, Frank. She was one of the most remarkable persons I ever knew. I could cry if I weren't so old myself, and fully aware that I shall be following

Prue in a few more years." Bascom tipped his coke bottle and took a long drink.

"How old are you, Bascom?"

"Away past sixty—more than halfway across the tightwire that stretches over the chasm of a normal lifetime, and I'm likely to lose my balance and fall off anytime. I guess that's why I don't feel much like crying about Prudence."

"Even Mom and my aunts didn't cry much while we were making all the funeral arrangements."

"Every age has its compensations, and one blessing is that the older you get the less you grieve about old people dying. The years squeeze out emotion and leave the spirit desensitized, just as they sap the juices of the flesh and leave it shriveled. Life has been lived; the show is over; and it is time to go home. Prue wouldn't want anyone crying at her funeral."

"No," I said, "she left instructions for everybody to have fun."

Bascom nodded. "She told me, the last time I saw her that she had seen so many sunrises that they didn't mean much to her any more, and that she was ready to take a look at another world, where there was no night."

"That's the way I feel, all right," Uncle LankyFrank said, "except I couldn't say it like she did."

"She bet me ten dollars once that she would outlive me."

Bascom's eyes were wide with wonder as they watched my hand reach back and get my billfold. I took out a ten-dollar bill.

"Here's the money."

He recoiled as though the bill had been presented by a ghost. "I can't accept that. I can't collect a bet from a dead woman. It was only a joke."

"She left written instructions for me to see that you

got the money. You can't refuse it, Bascom. Think about it...remembering and knowing Aunt Prue. You're afraid not to take it."

The look on Mr. Twog's face made me wonder if, in its plush-lined case in his right hip pocket, his famous madstone had given him a warning vibration. Bascom's madstone was known widely for its mysterious and occult powers. A Negro preacher, on his death bed in the attic of the Left Hand Hill Store, had given it to Bascom a long time ago. The dying preacher said he had taken it from the stomach of a deer he had killed at midnight, under a full moon, in a graveyard, down in Kentucky. It had proved its ability to help every ailment it had ever been tried on; had helped Bascom squirm through many ticklish situations. Boiled in sweet milk first, it was especially good for cuts, bruises and chigger bites.

Its story was one of the first shivery folklore yarns I ever heard when I was a kid. It made people behave themselves, solved all spiritual problems, settled love affairs. I knew now that it had been formed when the deer nibbled its mate's long winter hair, but I was enough of a hillbilly to wonder if it had prompted Bascom to act as he did.

Slowly his hand reached out for the money. His fingers shook, and he held the bill gingerly, passing it from one hand to the other, as though it were hot.

"It was a long time ago," he said thoughtfully. "She came in to buy some groceries one day. When I asked her by way of making conversation what her grocery bill was per month she said, 'It runs about three rolls of toilet paper.' She always bought the best grade of toilet paper. Called it Non-skid." Bascom's face was holy with earnestness. "So she remembered about the bet?"

"She left explicit instructions how she wanted her

funeral to be conducted."

"Hmm. Are you going to be able to comply with everything?"

"I think so. All except maybe the zither."

"Zither!"

"She wants *Turkey In The Straw* played on the zither. We don't know whether we can do that or not. We don't even know where we can find a zither, let alone anybody to play one."

Professor Twog got up hastily from the keg of nails he had been sitting on and went back along the narrow aisle between the counters stacked with merchandise, upstairs to his living quarters. In a minute or two he returned, carrying a highly polished zither in one hand and its ivory plectrum in the other. His eyes were moist, and when he spoke his voice was different—more subdued:

"This belonged to Maimie, my first wife. She died the same year we were married. She used to play it. I did, too, a little. But I haven't touched it in years." He rippled the plectrum exploringly across the strings. They tinkled softly, and Bascom felt his sad way through *My Old Kentucky Home* and *Swanee River*. "Maybe I could help you out."

"Go ahead," Uncle LankyFrank said. "I ain't heared one of them things for thirty years."

Bascom sat back down on the nail keg, with the zither across his knees. His right hand began a circular motion, as though he were pantomiming the turning of the handle of an old-fashioned coffee grinder, while his left hand sort of beat time, and lifting itself out of the way of the plectrum every time it saw the piece of ivory coming.

Turkey In The Straw is probably the best known hillbilly tune in America. At Spunky Ridge play parties and square dances it has emerged from every musical instrument the hill people could buy or invent, from piano to cornstalk fiddle. I've even heard it clogged with a shangle stick. It lifts spirits, stirs pulses, sets toes tapping.

At first Bascom played haltingly, feeling his way along. Then as the latent skill in his fingers broke from its long imprisonment, the turkey began to scratch straw for something to eat; and by the time the old tom-turkey had been fed all it could hold, and *Coony On A Rail* had practically walked his legs off, and the *Irish Washwoman* had finished her laundry, Bascom was bent over his zither, going after its music with both hands, like a man in a hurry picking fly specks out of pepper.

"You'll do it, then?" Uncle LankyFrank said, when Bascom finally stopped playing.

"I'll try," Bascom said. "For Prue — at her funeral — I'll try."

We left with the satisfaction that comes with having done a good day's work. "Wasn't that lucky?" Uncle LankyFrank said. "I didn't know Bascom had one of them things and could play it. I didn't even know he had been married once before, or that his woman had died. He come here around forty years ago, I guess — he was just a youngster — and bought the store from old man Hicks. Then he married Lizzie Morgan, as much to get away from the competition as anything else, some said."

"Yeah, I remember the Right Hand Hill Store," I said, "just across the road. Cohea Morgan ran it."

"When Cohea drownded in the Yorkynut Slough, Bascom married Lizzie and closed her store — only used it for a warehouse. It burnt along there some time before the first war and Bascom never did rebuild it."

"Wonder where Lizzie was today?"

"Sommers out in the Yorkynut, I guess, fishin'.

She's only at the store when Bascom wants to go someplace. Some say Lizzie still goes out lookin' for Cohea in the Yorkynut. They never did find him."

"Funny how you find out things about people, thataway and that," I said, "when somebody dies."

The more I thought about Aunt Prue the more I realized how much influence she had on the lives of people with whom she came in contact. If I didn't miss my guess, Professor Bascom Twog had been—or still was—in love with Aunt Prue, a woman twenty-five years his senior. Either that or what Rembrandt called Aunt Prue's witchery was doing its supernatural best —or worst—to provide fun at her funeral. As Mom said time after time, "What will people think, thataway and that: *Turkey In The Straw* played on a zither at sister Prue's funeral?"

It was getting dark when we got back to Saganois and reported to the others all that we had got done. Uncle LankyFrank and Aunt Birdella decided to drive back home that night—Wednesday—and come back Thursday morning, but would eat supper before they left.

Cousin Manford and his quiet, bulky wife, Edith, brought Aunt Maud and Uncle Parley Dooks over to Mom's house for supper, but Aunt Millie Dinnegan didn't feel like getting out of bed yet. We sat around the parlor after dinner, under the bird cages that had been covered for the night, and talked over all the plans we had made and couldn't think of anything we had forgot except the pallbearers, but there were plenty of youngsters of Dinnegan descent who would be at the funeral to take care of that job.

"Did Bonnie get here?" I asked Aunt Maud.

"Yes, but she didn't come out to the house."

"Why not? Where is she?"

"She got a room down at the hotel. Said she was going to work till midnight on the obit. I told her she could work on it out home as well as she could at the hotel, but she said not. Said she needed solitude or solicitude or something like that when she was writin'. I talked to her on the phone."

"Is Charles coming down for the funeral?"

"No, I guess not."

I knew Aunt Maud was waiting for me to ask about the insurance policy. "What did Bonnie say about the fifty thousand dollars?"

"I don't think you have to worry about that," Aunt Maud said nastily. "You won't get any of it."

"I'm not expecting any. What did Bonnie say about it?"

"Prue had one, all right, all paid up. Charles looked it up in the records. Bonnie said your name wasn't on it."

"Was hers?"

"She didn't say."

"Did she say anything about a will?"

"There's a will, too. Charles helped her make it out several years ago. We'll know all about it when the time comes."

The way Aunt Maud talked, she let on that she knew more than any of the rest of us knew about both the insurance and the will, and the old hatpin was enjoying her advantage.

"I think I'll go down and talk to Bonnie," I said.

"Not tonight," Aunt Maud said. "She's busy. She said you might upset her. She gets nervous when she's writin'."

By half past ten we had picked out the six pallbearers, and had made arrangements to haul the flowers, which would be stored in Gib Parker's funeral-home ice box until we were ready for them. Nothing else remained to be done, that we could think of, so everybody went home and Rembrandt and Mom and I were left by ourselves.

"Maud knows something," Mom said apprehensively. "Her and Bonnie and Charles have got things fixed just like they want them, thataway and that."

"You mean about the insurance and the will?" I asked.

"Yes, sir, and she ain't a-lettin' on. That bunch is after the money. Charles even called them folks out in Oregon to see if sister Prue had found any of that stuff she was looking for: You're rain' 'em, ain't it?"

"Had she found any?"

"No. She hadn't even opened the package that instroovment come in."

"Her Geiger counter?"

"No, that wasn't it."

"Scintillometer?"

"That's it. It was still in its box."

"I wouldn't worry about the money or anything else. I think Aunt Prue is running her own funeral and and everything connected with it."

"Aw, how could she?"

"Ask Rembrandt."

Brandy came over to where I was sitting and said, "Why don't you try to call Shawn? I've been trying to get her all evening, and I'm tired. Maybe you can get her now."

I went over to the phone and put in a long-distance call to our house in Windfall, and in a moment or two Shawn answered, "Hello."

"Hello, Shawn, how you getting along up there?"

"All right."

"Rem's been trying to get you all evening. Where you been?"

"Oh, Bill and I've been out rinkin' around. He just left."

"Work all day today?"

"Yes. I've been going like the devil was after me with his poker ever since you left last night."

"Stay by yourself last night?" Living in the country as we do, Rembrandt refuses to stay alone at night, but Shawn doesn't mind it.

"Oh, yes. I loaded the 97 and stood it behind the kitchen door, and took the 30-06 up to my room. Say, Boley, when did you get those 150-grain Silvertips?"

"Last fall. Why?"

"Nice looking cartridge. Looks like they might be pretty flat."

"They're around three thousand feet."

Roman and Fred both take after their mother, thank the Lord, but Shawn is more like me—likes the outdoors; guns and fishing and camping. I'd rather have her along on a big-game hunt than any man; and in a duck blind whenever I hear her shoot I know something is coming down. She shoots lefthanded, while I shoot from my right shoulder, which gives her the left front corner of the blind, an ideal arrangement. Her left eye is even larger and stronger than her right one, and when she sees meat in the air, her right eye grows smaller than ever, giving her an odd and attractive cockeyed look I never saw on any other woman.

"When did Winchester bring them out?" Shawn asked.

"They've been out quite a while. I just never got around to getting any. Did you try them?"

Whistle-pigs play along an old levee three hundred yards below our house, and sometimes—usually when Brandy has gone somewhere—Shawn and I slip out the upstairs window onto the roof of the back porch and pop a few primers at them.

"No, but I think I shall tomorrow, if things go like I have them aimed."

"The scope is set for them: Two inches high at a hundred yards, and on the nose at two hundred. You'll have to hold a little high on the groundhogs."

Brandy tapped me on the shoulder. "For Heaven's sake, ask her is she's coming down to the funeral Friday afternoon. Your three minutes are about up."

"You coming down for the funeral, Shawn?"

"I think so. Bill said he though we should."

I thought of Bill Tarsevik, the hog raiser. He would probably bring Shawn down in a new Cadillac. Then I happened to think of this other Bill — the log-hauling Bill. Dugan, his name was. Maybe Shawn hadn't taken Summer Street home yesterday morning, after all.

"By the way, which Bill you been rinkin' around with tonight?"

"Why do you ask that?"

"No reason particularly. I just thought—"

Shawn's voice tinkled like a wind-harp:

"The same one you would rink around with if you were me. Goodby."

8 Thursday morning the deluge started. It rained two inches by noon, and then the skies opened wide and it rained like a cow splattering on a flat rock. The downpour made those Spunky Ridge yellow-clay hills as soft and slick as chicken dobs, or *avian ordure*, as Aunt Prue might have commented after she was graduated from one of the colleges she attended during her long life.

The roads down in the southern half of Starbuck County were built chiefly for airplanes, and when it rains about the only way they can be traveled is on foot or with horses or mules. Roads in the north half of the county were all paved, but around Turtle Holler and Limberswitch there were quite a few shunpikes that that the farm-to-market, road-building program people apparently had not even been able to find.

I drove downtown to talk to Mr. Parker about the best way to meet this new problem of mud, and just as I stopped the car, Uncle LankyFrank pulled up behind me. We hustled inside the funeral home, which was still a furniture store, as it wouldn't be needed for the funeral, the way we had things planned.

"Ain't this somepn?" Uncle LankyFrank said.

"Sure is. Did you have any trouble getting out?"

"No, I can always go out through the back pasture

to the gravel, if I stay on the slab rock sticking out. Some of the rest of them that wanted to come — Black-Pete Rye and Matt Hicks and them — are going to have a hard time getting out though. Might have to put on ice creepers and hirple out."

"I don't know whether ice creepers would do much good in that yellow gumbo or not."

"They'd help."

"The main thing is, can Reverend Hoosh and Aunt Pop get out?"

"Oh, yeah, they can always come down Rocky Branch and up the river in their gas boat."

Mr. Parker came in from the back part of the store and said, "Good morning, folks. "I won't be able to get the hearse up Snake Mountain after all this rain. We shall have to plan some other way to get the coffin box from the road up to the cemetery."

It was a problem, all right. The main ridge of Spunky is five miles wide and about fifteen miles long, and Snake Mountain, on top of which the Dinnegan cemetery is located, is almost in the exact center of it. By using an old brush-hung road that still had a little gravel on it, we could drive from Saganois to the Spunky Ridge flag-stop, all right, and from there to the foot of Snake Mountain. Likewise the hearse would have no trouble getting from the Shake-Rag neighborhood to Spunky, over the Wild-cat road.

But in the mud, the hearse never could make it up to the top of the big hill. It was more than a quarter of a mile from the thin gravel up to the graveyard; even if you went straight up the side and didn't rounce the hill at all; and more than half a mile if you rounced around along the little old hint of a road that led up there. In any case, it was too far for the pallbearers to carry Aunt Prue, coffin, steel vault and all, even though they were all her young and husky grandnephews.

Mom and Rembrandt had come downtown with Cousin Manford Dooks and his folks—all but Aunt Maud—and the first thing Mom said was, "Ain't this a weary? All this rain." You could see that she was enjoying herself, wrestling with the problem. Everybody just stood around, thataway and that, thinking, and trying to find a good place to drip.

Mom kept chattering away, winding up with "Wonder how much Mr. Parker will charge us extry if we ruin his rugs?" After my Dad was shot, Mom for years had run a rooming house for railroad men and highbehinds, and she knew what a job it was to keep rugs looking nice.

"Don't worry about that, Mom," I said. "If you want to worry about something, worry about Bonnie. She hasn't finished the obit yet, Aunt Maud just told me."

The editor of the Saganois *Spotlight*, tall, gray-haired Mr. Stroud, came sloshing along past the funeral home and stopped to ask about the obituary. "The paper goes to press this morning," he said, "and I'd like to have it as soon as I could."

The Saganois *Spotlight* is a four-page weekly newspaper, read by practically everybody in the Spunky Ridge country. I had to tell Mr. Stroud that the obit wasn't ready yet—and the *Spot* came out that afternoon with a blank column in the middle of which was "Watch This Space Next Week for the Account of Mrs. Prudence Persnosky's Funeral."

I was so put out about the obit that I followed Mr. Stroud out the door and down the street to the Saganois Hotel and up its stairway to Bonnie's room and knocked on the door. Her typewriter was going so furiously that I had to knock two or three times, each time louder, and finally she stopped the racket and asked, "Who is it?"

"It's me. Boley."

She unlocked the door and let me in. She was a real fat overflowing woman. She overflowed at shoetops, girdle edges, frontispieces and several other places. Aunt Prue once observed that Bonnie would make a deep impression on a bathing beach even if she just sat still in the sand. I hadn't seen Bonnie for several years but the only change I noticed about her was more fat. Her once-blonde hair was the same swizzly gray, and she still had big blue eyes and that peach-bloom complexion that so many fleshy women have.

Before I could say anything about the obit she started raking me up one side and down the other:

"I suppose you think you're going to get some of Aunt Prue's money, just because you got a government job. Well, I got a letter from her awhile back, and the way she wrote she's going to leave some of it to me but not to you. All you're going to get is a dollar. Same way with the rest of them."

"Don't you think you should wait until the will is opened and read before you say anything like that?" I said. After all, I would put up my government job against her writing record any time.

"She found out you told stories and things about her. You even told around how she sneaked through the cornfield from the girls' outhouse at Shake-Rag and got behind the boys' privy and widened the cracks between the boards with her pocketknife."

I had to laugh. "It was Tom Larkey told that first—twenty-five or thirty years ago. They went to school together. Tom had a regular path over to the girls', and one recess they met on it."

"She said you told it."

"Even if I did, I don't believe Aunt Prue would hold that against me."

"You'll see."

It was something to be concerned about, all right. I hadn't seen Aunt Prue nor heard from her for a year or two, and she might have changed in her notions toward the last, thataway and that.

"Let's wait till the time comes before we start worrying about that. Right now we need the obit for the newspaper. How near done with it are you?"

"I'm up to where she was the hostess at that big hotel in Africa where the wild animals came out of the jungle at night to drink at the lake, and she lectured about them."

"Gee whiz, are you going to put all that in?"

"Certainly. It will be interesting to these hillbillies down here. But I can't seem to make it sound right."

I looked at the card table on which her portable electric typewriter sat. It was stacked with reams of white top-copy paper, yellow scratch sheets, carbon paper and onion skin, and more paper was arranged neatly in piles on the floor. The wastebasket was overfull and the bed was covered with copy she apparently thought was good enough to keep.

"Why don't you just say when and where she was born, whom she married, when and where she died, and let it go at that?"

"Oh, that wouldn't be consistent with my literary training. Even in writing an obituary it is necessary to follow certain rules of construction the same as in writing fiction, articles, or even photo-journalism."

"How is your writing career coming along, anyway?"

"Very well. My agent says I have the divine afflatus."

"The what?"

"Divine Afflatus. I wouldn't expect you to know what that is. You don't read writers' magazines or take writing courses."

"I'd have to look it up," I admitted.

"It's the writing spark. The Inspiration."

"Is that what you've been using on *Lost Moments* all these years?"

"Oh, yes."

"Which version of *Lost Moments* are you going to give to Aunt Pop to *give* at the funeral?"

"I had thought of permitting her to read my vignette, but I'm afraid it's not quite long enough. I guess I'll give her my *"Conte?"*

"That's French. I couldn't expect you to know what that is, either."

It was new to me, all right, but I didn't let on like it was. In such conversational contretemps I usually just say, "I think so, too," and snigger out of it with more or less embarrassment, but I couldn't say it now because it wouldn't fit, and would only expose my ignorance. "How big is your *conte*?" I asked.

"Oh, it's a little bit of a thing — only has three sides — but it reflects the same significant message."

It wasn't till I talked to Shawn that I learned what Bonnie meant with all her artistic talk. Shawn is active in Little Theater work, and she explained that in show business the pages of scripts to be memorized are called sides. So you can see what a puzzled and put out person I was at the time I talked to Bonnie. Not only was I ignorant of what a *conte* was, but also its three sides. I said to Bonnie, "You brought it along, of course."

"Oh, yes, I never go anywhere without it. One never knows when one will have use for it."

"Well, I guess that's taken care of then. And get the obit finished as soon as you can. The funeral's tomorrow afternoon, you know."

I went back to the funeral home and found a line of people waiting to sign the mourner's book that Mom was presiding over at Gib Parker's pulpit. Mom was in her glory, greeting friends and acquaintances she hadn't seen for years. They would step up, and as they signed their names, say, "No, we heard there was a funeral wreath on your door and thought we'd come down and see who it was for." And Mom would explain, "No, I thought I'd put one up, because my house was as much of a home as sister Prue ever had, thataway and that, the way she traveled all the time."

I went over to the corner of the room where Aunt Maud and Uncle LankyFrank and them were watching and listening.

"Bascom must have told it around how you paid him his ten dollars," Uncle LankyFrank said.

"How's that?"

"Ever'body thinks they're going to get ten dollars if they go to the funeral, and some think they'll get it if they just sign the griever's book."

I looked over at the slowly moving line. The people were laughing politely and having a good time telling half-forgotten stories about Aunt Prue. Just the few minutes I listened to them I heard about the time Aunt Prue threw Black-Pete Rye in a snowbank when he tried to waller her; the time she out-limbered Simon-Called-Peter Albans, the Turtle Holler part-time preacher's son—and him double-jointed, too—in a Limber Jim and shangle contest at Shake-Rag schoolhouse; and the time the big-city feller, Mr. Harrison Chandler, who had come down into the Spunky Ridge country to buy cedar trees for a big lead-pencil factory, was so shocked at what Aunt Prue did on the way home from a Sunday School picnic at Little Buck church. This last named, even I, who had quite a collection of Prudence Persnoskyalia, had never heard. I listened carefully:

"No, this feller Chandler," an old grizzled Spunky Ridge residenter with whiskers to his eyes was saying, "took Prue to the picnic, and she drank so much red lemonade that she got the scoots. Sycamore Boggs had hauled a bunch of boys and girls up to the picnic in his box wagon. Sycamore didn't have enough spring-seats to go around, so he just sawed some boards long enough to reach from one sideboard to the other and used them for seats. On the way home along about sundown Prue and this feller Chandler was ridin' on the back seat. They was comin' down Rocky Branch road, and it was rougher then than it is now even. Ridin' on the back seat, right above the hind wheels, Prue got the worst joltin' and it was a little too much for her."

I noticed Aunt Maud's thin lips crack in a smile that was a trifle more than just from the teeth out. She was hanging onto every word the old story-teller was saying. I thought it safe to ask her in a whisper, "Were you along that time?"

She nodded. "That red lemonade was something new. Prue just drunk too much of it."

"I remember that time," Uncle Parley said. "I was sparkin' you then."

"Shut up!" Aunt Maud said, "and listen."

"Well, sir," the bewhiskered old hillbilly said, "it didn't faze Prue a bit. She just waited till they come to the next bridge across Rocky Branch — you know how the road crosses the crik ever' little ways all the way down through Spooky Holler — and at the bridge she said she saw a wild rose she wanted to pick. The Chandler feller was goin' to get it for her, but she hopped the wagon before he could get around to it and and went in the brush and jerked off her pants and throwed them in the crick.

"Well, you know the next place where the road crossed the crick was the ford there by Ruff Morgan's place, where ever'body used to bring their buggies and warsh em. Prue hadn't more than got back in the wagon and was puttin' a wild rose in Mr. Chandler's buttonhole when they got to the Ford, and when they got right in the middle of it, with ever'body gawkin', here come Prue's pants floaten' down the crick."

"Who is that guy?" I asked Uncle LankyFrank.

"Note Spoon," Frank said. "Say, I just thought of somepn."

Mr. Spoon had paused to snicker, when he would have liked to bust out, you could see that, and then continued, "Fancy pants they was, too: white, and trimmed with blue lace. And you know them doggoned pants floated into the back wagon wheel and lodged agin a spoke, and the wheel brought them up and over, right past Mr. Chandler!

"Nobody said nothin', wantin' to be polite, thataway and that. But Prue she just up and yelled, 'three cheers for the red white and blue!'"

Mr. Spoon and his listeners laughed as heartily as they dared while standing in line to sign the griever's book, but the rest of us managed to keep our faces straight. After all, we had a funeral to hold and we wanted to conduct it in the most circumspect, time-honored manner. Aunt Prue, however, refused to let us do it that way.

"Note tellin' that yarn made me think of Tom Larkey," Uncle LankyFrank said. "He's got a team and wagon I think we could borry. Uses it to take town people on hayrides in summer, and hooks his team to a sled for 'em when it snows. Farms with a tractor mostly, but keeps Old Pete and Carrie Nation for these rides. Picks up quite a bit of change. He could meet the hearse at the foot of Snake Mountain and haul the coffin box up to the graveyard. The old folks and the preachers and maybe Gib Parker could ride along, but ever'body else would have to walk."

"Let's see," I said, "how many are there to ride: you and Aunt Birdella, Aunt Maud and Uncle Parley, Mom and Aunt Millie, Reverand Hoosh and Aunt Pop and Mr. Parker."

"Far's that's concened, I can hirple up. Tom would have to drive the team; and Till would want to go."

"Does Till still go around in the fur season offering to skin skunks and possums for ten cents apiece like she did when I was a kid?"

"No, she charges a quarter now—inflation, you know. Fifty cents for coons. She skun a coon and stretched its hide for Cohea Radison one day last winter and charged him a dollar for the two jobs."

"Till Larkey's quite an old bushwhacker," I said to Rembrandt. "Goes barefooted most of the time. Keeps a rock by the fireplace, and Tom told me once that her feet were so calloused that all she had to do to start a fire in the morning was jump out of bed and wham the rock with her heel and the sparks would start flyin', b'Desus!"

Brandy didn't appreciate the description. She was a town girl and never would make a good hillbilly.

"My woman Birdella is ailin' and maybe can't go, so that'll be one less to ride," Uncle LankyFrank said. "She's been ailin' since yesterday. I guess it was the funeral arrangements that upset her stomach. Anyway, she didn't feel like comin' up today."

We all expressed the hope that Aunt Birdella would get better soon and in time to attend the funeral, not only because we were really sympathetic, but because it was the polite and traditional thing to do. For down in my old home country of Spunky Ridge practically everyone is ailing practically all the time. However, most of the natives live to be eighty or ninety, and the chief reason they suffer ailments is to give them something to talk about besides the weather. Mostly they never let their ailments interfere with anything they really want to do. I myself have had a sore back all my life but I never pay any attention to it except when I find it convenient so to do.

After taking time out for Aunt Birdella's indisposition we resumed our discussion of Uncle LankyFrank's idea and finally decided it would work out all right. "Get your car, Boley," Frank said, "and we'll go out to Tom's and see what he says."

"Will we need chains?"

"No, that road splashes some, but there's enough gravel left on it to keep us from droppin' out of sight."

Tom and Till Larkey lived out beyond Sny Magrew. Their house sat right on top of Happy Rock Hill. The Dinnegan cemetery was only three miles from the Larkey place, so Tom wouldn't have but six miles to go altogether. The deal looked good if we could swing it. "Keep your toes crossed," Uncle LankyFrank said.

We found Mr. Larkey shelling seed corn in the driveway of his barn. He was as lanky-limber as any hillbilly you ever saw, narrow between the eyes, and as shriveled as Uncle Parley Dooks but far from being as feeble. In fact, he didn't even wear glasses. He talked in a kind of chunking, nasalm banjo-string twang. When he looked up and saw me, he twanged, "Well, if it aint' Boley. I knowed it was rainin' hard, but I didn't think it was rainin' *that* hard."

"Hello, Tom. Glad to see you. Where's Till?"

"Out huntin- mushrooms, b'Desus."

"In this rain?"

"Warm as it is, they're poppin' up all the time."

Next to my Uncle LankyFrank, Tom Larkey is my favorite hillbilly. He tought me so many interesting things to do in the country when I was a kid that I can't begin to list them. I was only three when my Dad was shot, so I can't remember having a father to teach me what to a boy are the most important lessons. After my Dad was killed, and Mom moved to Saganois and started her rooming-house, I spent all my school vacations in Spunky Ridge, living part of the time with Uncle LankyFrank and Aunt Birdella and the rest with Tom and Till Larkey. It was Tom who taught me to "read the woods," as he called it: to locate bee trees, fishing holes and fox dens; to recognize the track of a coon, possum, mink, skunk, fox or any other denizen of the woods when I saw it; to skin and clean game, roll it in thick clay mud and roast it in the hot coals of a camp fire, then wash it down with spring water; to set a box trap, steel trap or deadfall; to make elderberry wine, and hunt Morel mushrooms, ginseng and Indian Turnip. The hillbillies had many ways of earning a meager livelihood, and I was familiar with them all.

It was good to see Tom. The three of us sat around a battered washtub and shelled ear corn into it by hand, saving only the kernels that would be sure to sprout, and talked about the old days for awhile. Then Uncle LankyFrank said, "Prue died the other day out in Or'gon and we're goin' to bury her tomorrow in the Dinnegan cemetery."

"I heared about it," Tom said softly. "I and Till was talkin' last night. We feel kinda glad about it—wisht we was goin' with her. When you get up past eighty it's kinda nice to know that you aint a-goin' to have to fight much longer. That Prue fit a good fight."

Down here in the middle of my old home country, amidst the sources of folklore, superstition and honest ignorance, I found it easy to say, "You know, Tom, I think Aunt Prue is holding her own funeral. I don't think we are having anything to do with it. Some of the oddest and funniest things have happened."

We told Tom some of the outlandish requests Aunt

Prue had made, and when we mentioned the zither, Tom slapped his bony knee and said, "That's Prue for you—*Turkey In The Straw* on a zither! She was a faunchy one."

We were sitting on bales of oats straw, and sixteen feet away a cricket on the floor of the driveway was drowned in a sea of snoose juice shot from Tom's pursed lips. "I'll never forget Prue tellin' how hard she worked to get you to ask your woman to marry you, Frank," Tom said. "It was at the log-rollin' over at Shake-Rag schoolhouse, after ever'body had went home—ever'body except the young folks, that is. You and Birdella was settin' close together on a log, sparkin' in the dark, but you couldn't get up nerve enough to ask her. Prue said she got a mullien'weed stalk and snuk up behind you and started ticklin' first one and then the other. You thought it was Birdella ticklin' you, and Birdella thought it was you ticklin' her; and between the two of you, you got the job done."

Tom had another moment of merriment, and then his face straightened. He knew what we had come for; knew that the idle, nostalgic talk was merely the necessary, traditional overture preceding request for a favor; was aware of the touchiness of hillbilly pride. "How are you going to get that heavy hearse up Snake Mountain in this mud?"

"That's what we wanted to see you about," Uncle LankyFrank said. "We thought maybe you could haul the coffin box up in your tight wagon. Leave the hearse at the foot of the hill. I guess the box wagon would be better than the hay rack. Look a little better."

"I and Till have thought about it. I'll hitch Old Pete and Carrie Nation up and meet you there. What time?"

"It'll be between three and half past, I reckon," Uncle LankyFrank said, "by the time we get ever'thing straightened out, thataway and that."

"I got some spring-seats for Molly and them, and I got a tarp I can put up if it keeps on rainin'—and it looks like it will."

On the way back to Saganois Uncle LankyFrank and I went over our plans again, and it seemed we had everything taken care of, even if it kept on raining. There was even a tent over the grave the Barnes boys had dug the day before, a tent that Uncle LankyFrank had bought at the auction of the effects of a carnival company that had gone broke at the Saganois Forty-second Annual Free Fish Fry & All Week Carnival a few years ago. "Don't know why I bought it," Frank said. "Hung it in the barn loft on a balin' wire so the mice couldn't get to it, and never did use it. I guess it was a good idy, puttin' it up in all this rain, over the grave thataway and that. Git all the dirt and grease warshed offen it."

"It was a lucky break that you had that tent," I said. "Mr. Parker said he had just the one tent, and it was out at Puckerbrush at his other funeral."

So we were all ready—we thought. However, Aunt Prue still had a whole hatful of tricks left. For that night, down at the funeral home where we all gathered for a final conference, the phone rang and the call was for me:

"Hello, this is Boley Paydoley."

"This is Stambo, Pistol River, Oregon."

"Yes."

"The court out here opened the envelope containing Mrs. Persnosky's will this morning with the intention of taking the first steps in processing it. You remember I mentioned the will as having been found in her big pocketbook together with some other papers."

"Yes."

"Well, the envelope contained a second envelope with the will in it. Also there was a letter requesting that the will be read at her funeral, while everbody is still present and can hear it. That is a very unusual request."

"That doesn't surprise me at all," I said. "That's nothing compared to some of the other stunts she's asked for."

"She must have been a most remarkable person."

"That's putting it mildly." I looked across the room at Rembrandt. "I think she was a witch. Did she say who was to read it?"

"You, if possible; otherwise, Mrs. Bonnie Dooks Stabbs."

"I don't think either of us will be able to do it, because we won't have it. The funeral's tomorrow. It won't have time to get here."

"I mailed it to you in care of Mr. Parker at Saganois this morning, right away after the top letter was opened. I sent it Air Mail Registered Special Delivery."

I groaned. "You shouldn't have registered it. Registered mail travels in prescribed channels, for reasons of safety, and signatures are required every time it changes hands enroute. If you hadn't registered it, it would have a chance of getting here in time, but now I don't think it'll make it."

"The court advised me to mail it to you, and you are to return it here after the funeral."

"I hope it gets here in time, but if it doesn't we'll just have to go ahead and hold the funeral without it."

"I'm sorry that we didn't get around to opening that letter a day sooner."

"That's all right. Thanks for letting us know, anyway, and for doing your best."

"And thank you, Mr. Paydoley, so much."

I hung up the receiver and looked at Bonnie, who had taken time out from writing the obit to come over from the hotel and join the rest of us for the conference at the funeral home. She wore a possum-eatin'-poultry grin.

"Aunt Prue is at it again," I said. "She wants either Bonnie or me to read the will at the funeral."

"Now you'll see who's right," Bonnie said. She flounced out the door and down the street toward the hotel, going faster than I ever saw her go before or since.

9 Tom Larkey proved to be right when he said it looked like it would keep on raining. When we got up Friday morning it was still pouring as hard as it had been Thursday morning. According to the weather report a high-pressure front from the east and a low-pressure front from the west had collided in a super-middle-pressure double front that obviously centered on Starbuck County. We could imagine how slick the yellow-clay gumbo would be on the slab rocks that jutted out of the sod every few feet on the rouncing road up Snake Mountain. When Uncle LankyFrank suggested it would be best if everyone wore creepers on their boots and overshoes, the same as they did when it was icy underfoot, there was a big run on the Saganois stores that handled mud hooks and currycomb ice creepers. Stores that sold raincoats and gum boots had run out of these items the day before, and had ordered more, but they wouldn't arrive until noon, on the main-line train from Chicago.

Everybody I talked to Friday morning planned to attend the funeral, even though they knew they would have to climb Snake Mountain in the mud. The news that the will would be read at the cemetery caused the people to think their names might be mentioned in it, particularly if they remembered ever doing any little favor for Aunt Prue. They would take no chances of missing out by staying at home; they would go to the funeral rain or shine. Hard telling what was in that will. So they not only signed Mom's mourner's book, but bought raincoats, gum boots and creepers; and for two days Aunt Prue's funeral made better business in Saganois than the town had enjoyed in a coon's age.

I met The Folly when she got in and asked Sub Scott if he had handled a registered letter from Pistol River, Oregon, coming down. He looked at his records. "No, sir, Mr. Paydoley, I didn't. I had twenty-six coming down, but none from there."

"It's my aunt's will. It might come in either from Chicago or St. Louis, depends on which plane it got on out there. Let's take a look at your air-line schedules — TWA or United. Pistol River is on a star route, I think, and air mail from there would have to get over to the Eureka coast-line railroad, or else to the Portland & San Francisco RPO down through Dunsmuir and Red Bluff. It would head east on a plane out of either Portland or Frisco — maybe Oakland."

We didn't have a mail-sorting scheme for any state as far away as Oregon was, so we couldn't figure out exactly how the letter would come. "Well, keep looking for it," I said. "I'll meet the Chicago train, and the one from St. Louis that the corpse comes in on, and if it doesn't get here on either one, it's just too bad,"

When 58 from Chicago got in I swung up into the mail car and asked the register clerk if he had an air-mail special for Saganois. "It's from Pistol River, Oregon."

"Never heard of the place," he said. "I suppose you're after its postmark for your collection."

"Not exactly — I already have one. But if the letter I'm looking for gets here I'll have a spare. It's got a will in it."

The register clerk — Mort Simpson, it was — stood twirling his mail keys at the end of their long brass dog chain in the traditional highbehind manner, describing a figure 8 in the air. Around depots you can always identify highbehinds by the dog chains on their hips and by the official badges, that look as though they were cut out of the tops of tomato cans, they have to wear. They also wear snub-nosed, 38-caliber pistols — or are supposed to, at least — except that most of the weapons are worn in pigeonholes in letter cases, once the train leaves the station.

I climbed back down the mail-car steps, turned around, and there standing under the train shed out of the rain was Mr. Charles Willard Stabbs, guarding an enormous suitcase.

"Hello, Bolander," he said in his cold, deep, precise voice.

Even in a raincoat he was a fancy-looking man: Wore a Homburg hat and an elegant suit, and the knot in his necktie was a perfect funnel.

"Hello, Cousin Charles. I understood you weren't coming down for the funeral."

When I shook hands with him I felt for the calloused places on his knuckles. They weren't there, so I knew he had been promoted since the last time I saw him and didn't have to go around knocking on doors any more in order to colllect weekly life-insurance premiums.

"That was only a jest I foisted on Bonnie." He chuckled pompously. "Aunt Prue was one of my favorite relatives."

Suddenly I knew the reason for Bonnie's big hurry the night before, as well as the reason why Charles had come. Bonnie had hurried to telephone him from the hotel when she learned that Aunt Prue's will wouldn't arrive in time for the funeral.

Aunt Maud had said that Charles worked in the section of his insurance company that helped people make their wills, so he undoubtedly had access to a copy of Aunt Prue's Last Will & Testament. Probably he had it in his pocket now. When the time came he would hand it to me with one of his pompous flourishes. Then, aware of its contents, he would bow politely, step back and grin like a possum eatin' poultry.

It would make no difference to anybody, of course, whether the original will or a copy of it was read. By this time, however, I was afraid to deviate even a blonde hairsbreadth from Aunt Prue's instructions. If I did she would likely rise up out of her coffin and chounce me.

I looked down at Cousin Charles; neatly pressed trouser cuffs — no twog in them, I'd bet — and his high-shine shoes, and wondered what they would look like after he had mudded it up Snake Mountain. "We've run into quite a few problems, getting ready for the funeral," I said. "One is the prospect of climbing a big hill in the mud. All but the old folks are going to have to walk. You better get some boots and some other clothes."

"I have them here." He nudged his suitcase with his tow. "I anticipated the conditions, and brought the apparel I wear when watching birds."

"Watching...birds?"

"Yes, I am a charter member of a prominent Chicago Bird-Watching group. The *Alta Pete* Society."

I had heard of bird-watchers but had never met any except the ones who watched birds through the bottoms of highball glasses instead of field glasses, and found birds like the White-Fronted Pushover and the Furtive Nut-Scratcher of more than usual interest. I didn't want to reveal my ignorance by asking what *Alta Pete* meant. It sounded like Latin to me, and when I got around to looking it up, sure enough it *was* Latin. It means Seek Thou High Things, which I consider an excellent name for a bird-watching society.

I was humming and hawing around, trying to think of something to say that would not reveal my ignorance, when Charles saved me by asking, "In preparing for the last rites did you encounter difficulties with the relatives or were they all acquiescent? I can't imagine my mother-in-law agreeing to anything without a controversy."

"Not too many," I said. "But we probably would have if Aunt Prue hadn't taken things into her own hands and left us all those instructions. What got into her, do you think?"

"The instructions were not unique in any respect. Similar requests are processed by my company quite often. The American longevity tables are rising steadily, and as they rise such requests and instructions appear with increasing frequency in both insurance policies and Wills & Testaments. Particularly is this true in the Octogenarian Plus category, and more particularly on the distaff side."

"I think so too," I said, and sniggered out by asking Charles if I could give him a lift down to the Saganois Hotel. He said I could, and then I told him I would be glad to have him and Bonnie ride out to the foot of Snake Mountain with Mom and Rembrandt and me. He said he appreciated the offer and would be ready.

By noon we had done everything we could think of to hold as dignified a funeral as we could under the unusual circumstances. Mr. Parker had hired Latrum Squall to haul the grass, flower racks and interring equipment up to the foot of Snake Mountain in a truck. Two of the pallbearers had gone along to help carry the load up the mountain and set it under Uncle LankyFrank's tent that he had bought so cheap from the gone-bust carnival company, so everything was ready at that end.

Latrum's eyes rolled spookily as he reported that the hard rain had washed some of the dirt and grease off the canvas, and that he could make out the likeness of a lady with a loop of beads around her neck and also some words, but I didn't pay him any mind at the time, I was so concerned with other and more important matters.

Besides, I remembered how spooky he acted around the depot whenever a corpse was wheeled across the platform, keeping his mail cart as far away from it as possible. When I asked him how was the road up the big hill he said it was as slick as axle-grease, and to be sure that everybody wore their creepers if they intended to hirple up to the graveyard. "Are you going to the funeral?" I asked Latrum. "N-no," he stammered, "I have to stay and take care of the United States mails."

Mom closed her mourner's book at noon and went home to help Mrs. Plink fix a bite of lunch for anybody who happened to drop in, but the big mourner's meal would not be served until after the funeral. Mom had laid in a supply of ham and chicken and other grub. We would probably be late getting back, and Mom said we might as well eat supper at her house before we started home.

"What'll you do, Boley," she asked, "if that will aint on No. 57?"

"We'll just have to go ahead without it."

Mom pursed her lips disapprovingly. "I tell you, I don't like the way Bonnie and them are actin'. When I saw Charles come in to sign the book I thinks, thinks I, you old rip, you wouldn't be down here if you didn't know somepn we don't know. Just because he married Bonnie he thinks he's in the family, thataway and that. But actin' like he is, he aint *in,* he's *out.* I just bet he's got a copy of the will and he'll want you to read it."

"I thought about that, too, but what of it? One copy is the same as the other."

"Maybe it is and maybe it aint. Hern might be different. You just wait and see, he'll want you to read hisn."

"That's all I can do if the original doesn't get here."

"Well, it aint the way sister Prue said to do, thataway and that."

Cousin Manford Dooks was appointed Parade Master, and Gib Parker had given him a big bundle of White flags he was to put on the cars lined up for the funeral procession. Manford was a volunteer fireman, owned a good waterproof fireman's coat and hat, and so was the right man for the job. The cars carrying the flower girls and flowers would go first, followed by those hauling the nearer relatives, and tailing out with the hot-rods and sport cars of the young grandnieces and grandnephews.

Then would come the friends and neighbors, and the hopeful people who thought there was a chance of hearing their names mentioned when the will was read. Although we wouldn't have a hearse for Aunt Prue, who was going to ride The Folly most of the way, we certainly were going to give her a grand funeral cortege.

Long slender lances of rain were still stabbing the ground, but the water wasn't coming down quite as recklessly as it had been for the last twenty-four hours: Like a cow splattering—about like a calf. Along with a gun or two, I always carry my duck-hunting parka and hip boots in the trunk of my car, so right after lunch I got into them and was ready for the foulest weather.

Rembrandt had bought a new, dark-blue nylon rain outfit, complete with boots to match; and Mom, who was going to ride up Snake Mountain in Tom Larkey's box wagon, had her big black old-fashioned parasol. We all got ready around one o'clock and drove down to the hotel to pick up Bonnie and Charles.

Saganois will never forget Mr. Charles Willard Stabbs and his all-weather bird-watching costume. When he came out of the hotel lobby to get in my car everybody stopped in their tracks and stared at him. Shades were raised, moisture rubbed from window panes; and eyes popped with fascinating interest.

He wore a tight-fitting, fiery-red rubber jacket that had a brilliant green patch pocket for binoculars built onto its left breast, and a pair of gleaming white rubber pants that reached up to his armpits. The pants had feet in them. On his head was a bright yellow fez with a roof at the back, and a bushy black tassel six or eight inches long. The fex had "Alta Pete" embroidered in a flourish across its front. The costume was a pretty good rain outfit at that, except it didn't drain the water off his face very well—just the second or two it took him to cross the sidewalk and get in my car I noticed drops of rain clinging to his itchy-gitchy mustache—but it looked rather odd at a funeral.

Bonnie wore galoshes and a long raincape of white plastic. She looked like an elongated baloon, inflated to the no-wrinkle stage. "Isn't Charles a fine-looking thing to be going to a funeral?" she asked, after she had wedged her way into the car.

"I would have worn my raincoat over this admittedly blatant regalia," Charles said, "if you would have agreed to omit your ridiculous *Lost Moments* from the funeral rites."

"I can't do that, Aunt Prue insisted."

"I am well aware of your aunt's distorted sense of so-called humor. You, however, are not. Your super-egotism will not permit you to understand the real reason why your aunt requested such a stultiloquy. My costume is no more absurd than your *Lost Moments* travesty."

"But you look silly."

"Likewise, your *Lost Moments* sounds silly. My offer, for your information, is still open. I have my raincoat."

"I refuse to do it."

"Very well."

They argued all the way to the depot and were still at it when Cousin Manford waved me to the head of the procession, next to his own car. I was surprised to see Saganois Street lined with cars on both sides for four blocks. Cousin Manford didn't have nearly enough little white flags for all the cars.

I got out and sloshed over to where The Folly was spotted in her customary place. Wild Ike Highspeed Skaderight was warming up her engine and two depot men were loading a few pieces of express. Train 57 from St. Louis was due in ten minutes, and then we could transfer Aunt Prue and take off.

I climbed up into the baggage compartment where old man Skates was supervising the loading of his car. "Got Lupe and Chiquita going back to Vinton," Skates said, and nodded at two burros tied by their halter ropes, one at each end of the thirty-foot space. "That makes three times I've hauled them to the jacks this spring but I guess they got stuck for sure this time — they aint faunchin' like they was when I hauled 'em down last week. Cute, aint they? Gentle as dogs, too, now that they're stuck. That's why the fellers from the stud farm didn't bother to put 'em in their crates." He pointed at the crates, stacked on on top of the other, in a front corner of the car.

"Good idea," I said, "tying one at each end of the car. That way you'll have more space for the coffin box. Set it here on the left side next to the door so we can get at it right away as soon as you stop at Spunky."

The burros were old friends of The Folly crew, having made several trips from Vinton down to the stud farm at Saganois every spring for four or five years. They had always been reluctant to "take" a jackass, however, and were faunchy till they "took." Now, however, having spent a week at the stud farm, where their meager urges apparently had been satisfied, they were content and contemplative as they munched their wisps of hay.

I went over and scratched Chiquita's ear, and she drew back her big thick lips and grinned. "Hello, Lupe," I greeted the mule at the other end of the car, and she switched her tail in answer.

The Folly doesn't carry much express — and practically no baggage — on the north-bound-trip. Outside of three empty chicken coops, half a dozen crates of eggs and twelve or fifteen cans of milk for the dairy at Windfall, there wasn't anything in the car except the two burros and their crates, Lou Skates' arm chair and the steel chest he locked remittances up in.

I checked over everything I could think of again, and was sure we had complied with all of Aunt Prue's requests. Reverend Hoosh and his daughter Aunt Pop Papp, although it had been necessary for them to come up the Saganois River in their gas boat, were on hand, the two girls who were to sing *Shall We Gather At The River* were ready to both sing and gather, and I saw Bascom Twog with his zither in a waterproof sack standing under the train shed.

Main-line 57 doesn't stop at Saganois unless it has a passenger to drop off, or one to get on, but only slows down so its highbehinds can heave out-going mail through the door, and then snatch a hanging pouch with the catcher arm on its mail car. Today, however, it had Aunt Prue — and stopped twice: Once at the regular passenger crossing, and again when the engineer had to spot the door of the baggage car at the hand-truck crossing.

The train was right on the advertise. She pulled in, the door of the baggage car slid back, and there was Aunt Prue. The express-room boys loaded the coffin box on their truck and trundled it around to where The Folly was spotted.

Mom and my aunts shed a few tears as Aunt Prue was wheeled slowly across the depot platform, but there was no real weeping. Mom had told it around that Aunt Millie would be the one who would break down and take it hard if anybody would, but Aunt Millie didn't even chunk her arms up and down. Mom had brought along extra handkerchiefs and a bottle of camphor if anybody needed them, but nobody did—except maybe Latrum Squall, who stood waiting with his mail cart at the far end of the platform, and who looked like he could use a whiff of camphor.

It is an iron-clad rule of the Burlington Route that no coffin box can be set directly on the drain boards of a baggage or express car, but must rest on something. Drain boards are installed to catch drippings from heat-exploded milk cans, livestock, and shipments of liquids that might spring a leak; and the railroad company does not want to risk staining or damaging a coffin box in any way. So four or five rollers, supplied for the purpose, were placed under Aunt Prue, and splinters were wedged under the rollers to keep them from rolling backwards or forwards when the engineer started or stopped the train.

As soon as 57 stopped I climbed into its mail car and asked about the letter I was expecting. I had my mail keys on my hip, and if 57 had brough the letter I was going to open the Saganois pouch right there on the platform in the presence of Latrum Squall and get it.

However, the register clerk said he hadn't dispatched any registers at all to Saganois. "I guess there's no use opening it, then," I told Latrum, but I don't think he heard me, the way his eyes were wide and bugging as he watched Aunt Prue being unloaded.

The only thing I could do now was ask Charles if he had a copy of the will with him, and if he didn't we would just have to do without it. Aunt Prue had passed away too far away, and that was all there was to it.

I went back to The Folly and checked the way-bill that was pasted on the end of the coffin box, just to be sure Aunt Prue was inside—I wasn't going to take a chance on anything or trust anybody, the way everything had been going. It was all right: The weight was 850 pounds, steel vault, coffin and all, and a card on the end of the Box beside the way-bill read, "REMAINS OF MRS. PRUDENCE PERSNOSKY, SAGANOIS, ILLINOIS."

Finally I had a word with substitute Scott. "Stick your head in through the escape door under the letter case once in a while, if you have time, and see how things are going in the baggage car, will you, Scotty? Old man Skates doesn't have any respect for coffin boxes, he's hauled so many of them, and he'd as soon as not sit on my aunt to eat his second lunch."

"I'll do that, Mr. Paydoley."

"He always eats his second lunch between Sny Magrew and Limberswitch, and I don't want any coffee stains or hard-boiled egg yolks on the coffin box. I cautioned him, but he might forget."

It was fifteen minutes before The Folly was due to leave town, which gave us that much head start on her in getting up to Spunky Ridge. Everything was working out very well. The procession left Saganois, and although there was no hearse leading it, everybody noticed the flags on the cars and let us have the right of way even without turning our headlights on.

Rembrandt was worried about Shawn. "I can't understand what that girl means. I know she intended to come."

"Maybe The Clunker drowned out, or maybe she and Tarsevik are married and off on their honeymoon by now," I said helpfully. "You never know what these modern kids will do. Maybe she'll meet us at Spunky or even the cemetery."

"She wouldn't get married," Brandy said. "She might get engaged, Bill had such good luck with his hogs. But not married."

"You haven't met this other Bill, have you—Bill Dugan, the one she hauled to town?"

"Of course not. I don't think she's interested in him. She didn't say anything about him to me Tuesday."

"I don't know. Remember what she told me the other night on the telephone."

"Yes, but that was probably just to keep you guessing, like she's done with you all her life."

"Don't sell this Bill Dugan guy short."

"If she isn't at the funeral I'm going to try to call her right afterward."

"I wouldn't bother—we'll start home right after supper."

"You forget she's stayed three nights by herself now."

"Don't worry," I said reassuringly, "she's got the shotgun downstairs and the rifle upstairs; and there's the yard lights and the dogs—the way she shoots I'd hate to think what anybody would look like after she took a few shots at him—or even his car—if he tried any funny business."

I wasn't worried about Shawn. She was a typical young American girl, smart, sophisticated, able to take care of herself under any circumstances. Once when she was about twelve I asked her what she would do if she should suddenly find herself in some foreign country, without money, passport or any kind of identification. She replied, "I'd look up the American consul, explain the infield-fly rule to him, and order him to send me home. But first I'd call you on the trans-ocean telephone."

I wasn't concerned about Shawn, but the will was something else. I told Bonnie, "I guess neither of us will read the will. Nothing came in. I checked both trains."

"Oh, I don't know."

Charles' voice was smug. "I have a copy with me."

I feigned the utmost surprise. "You do?"

"I brought a copy along in the event it would be needed."

"You must know all about it then. Who gets the Cadillac?"

"That is difficult to ascertain with any relative degree of certainty. The will is quite complicated. Suffice to say it contains many surprises."

"We could read it now," Bonnie suggested eagerly, "just to us here in the car."

"No!" Mom put her foot down. "You'll read it right there at sister Prue's grave like she said."

"I guess that will be the best," I said. "You know, Charles, I'm afraid not to follow Aunt Prue's instructions as closely as we can."

Charles grunted condescendingly, and I didn't say any more.

At the Spunky Ridge flag stop everything went like clockworks. The hearse came in from the west right ahead of the funeral procession, just as The Folly honked her air horn for the station. There was a hand truck on the cindered platform, left there for dairy farmers to set their milk cans on, and we had to load

Aunt Prue on it first and then wheel her over to the hearse, so I jumped out in the rain and got it in place just as the train stopped. Lou Skates slid back the door of the baggage car, and I noticed he had a dazed look, was puffing hard and rubbing his left hip, but I didn't pay no mind at the time.

If we had thought to analyze the situation completely we might have guessed that because we didn't have the right will to read, Aunt Prue would pull some kind of ghostly trick to see that we did. But it was raining cats and dogs and we wanted to get her loaded into the hearse as soon as we could so we could get back in our cars where it was dry.

"Well, Lou," I said brightly, "you got here, all right, in spite of the rain."

Mr. Skates' conductor's cap was gone, and so were his spectacles. His bib overalls were smeared with a whitish-yellow slime, and he was so poohed-out that he could only babble hoarsely. I could make out very few words: "Rain," "school-teachers" and "egg ," I recollect him saying; and something about jackasses and "that gawd-dam' trickle valve," and "get this thing out of here before it kills me!"

I figured the rubber-kneed old fellow had met with some minor difficulty, perhaps when he had thrown the switch for the back-up into Sny Magrew, but I didn't take time out in all the rain to find out what. He helped Cousin Manford and me to push the coffin box out onto the truck, then sort of slid backward and sat down, utterly exhausted, on a chicken coop. He didn't even slide the door back shut.

As soon as I looked at the coffin box I knew Mr. Skates had disregarded my request and had eaten his second lunch on Aunt Prue. However, it was raining so hard that by the time we got the thing in the hearse all the egg stains had been washed off, and I didn't think anybody noticed them except myself. Nevertheless, I decided to chounce Lou about it when I ran with him on my next tour of duty.

Tom Larkey with his wagon box was waiting at the foot of Snake Mountain, and it didn't take us long to get Aunt Prue loaded in under the tarpaulin out of the rain. The coffin box slid in under the spring-seats nicely, clearing them about a foot. Tom fastened the endgate and we were ready to start up the hill.

A farm-wagon spring-seat is something you hardly ever see any more except in a museum. It is a flat board, as long as the wagon bed is wide, with a leaf spring at each end. The springs have hooks, which hook over the top of the sideboards. Other narrower boards are fastened to the main seat to provide a low back rest for the occupants and to keep them from sliding off the ends at sidling places. Tom had five of them.

Because he was the driver of Old Pete and Carrie Nation, Tom sat in the front spring-seat, on the right-hand side, with his wife Till beside him. Till was a big waddling woman, much heftier than Tom, so her side of the seat rode about a foot low.

Tom was a stickler for keeping the weight divided evenly on his wagon, so in the second seat he sat Mom and Aunt Millie. Mom was a lot heavier than Aunt Millie, so Tom sat her right behind him to make a good balance, which hoisted Aunt Millie so high she could look over the top of Till's head. Behind her sat squabby Uncle Parley, whose nose was about level with Aunt Millie's seat, and beside him was Aunt Maud, who reared up a foot higher. In the fourth seat were Aunt Pop Papp and Reverend Hoosh, their weights, heavy and light, distributed the opposite way; and in the last seat were crowded Uncle Lanky-Frank, Aunt Birdella—who had recovered rapidly from her ailment—and Mr. Parker, the undertaker. So loaded, the spring-seats resembled a cubistic design of a stairway, and the wagon itself looked top heavy and as though it might sway. It didn't though.

Lined up right behind the wagon were the second living generation of relatives—the ones in their fifties and sixties. Then came those in their thirties and forties, with the youngsters bringing up the rear. The six young and husky pallbearers were to walk along, three on each side of the wagon, and try to keep the mud pushed out from between the spokes of the wheels so it wouldn't ball up and make that much more weight for the horses to pull. Cousin Manford was the field marshal for this arrangement, and I gave him great credit for the good job he had done.

Cousin Bonnie and Charles were beside Rembrandt and me and the other closer relatives, right behind the wagon.

"Have you seen Shawn?" Rembrandt asked.

"No, but she's probably around here somewhere, probably back with the youngsters. She wouldn't get her until the last minute, anyway, you know Shawn."

"I've been watching all the cars as far as I could see in all this rain down the road, but I haven't seen The Clunker."

"Tarsevik will probably bring her down. They'll come straggling up the hill about the time we get up there."

Bonnie was still working on the obit, but how she was going to make any changes in it without getting it soaked I didn't know. She asked me, "Would you say 'her father was a drummer boy' in the Civil War, or just 'played a drum'?"

"Don't ask me. I was behind the door when divine afflatus was passed around." I was disgusted with her.

"It doesn't sound quite right to say 'boy' when he was

such an *old* man when he died. And would you say 'War Between The States' instead of 'Civil War?' I know there's two schools of thought on that."

"Either one," I said. "But you better decide pretty quick. We're going to need the obit in a few minutes."

Tom Larkey waited until everybody got their mudhooks on, then called out from his high seat, "Well, I guess we might as well start. It's going to get late on us now."

He shook the lines out over the horses and yelled above the rain pattering on the tarp, "Yup, there! Pete! Carrie! Shiddahoo! Yup!"

The big draft animals leaned against their collars as they tested the load. Then their powerful leg muscles bulged, their tails popped up as they strained, snorted, f....., and the wagon started.

The hint of a road that led up to the cemetery zigzagged in rounces to make the going easier, but at that the horses couldn't go more than a few yards at a time without stopping to catch their breath. The sparks flew whenever their sharp-shod hoofs raked across a jut of slab rock, and clouds of steamy vapor rose from the rain streaming down their sweating sides. The wagon was as near being a chariot of fire as a person ever sees on earth, and Aunt Prue was ascending in it. I considered this a fitting thing, something my fabulous aunt would appreciate and would thank us for after she arrived in Heaven.

We were about halfway up the mountain, at the steepest part, when I heard a slithering, ghostly sound, something like trees rubbing against each other on a dark and windy night. I glanced up and saw a tiny crack appear in the endgate. On the steep slope the coffin box had slid against it and was pressing hard.

The crack widened and the endgate bulged. I thought frantically, will she hold or won't she? Then just as I yelled WHOA! the endgate let go and the heavy coffin box came sliding out and banged against a slab of rock. The upper end held together, and remained leaning against the wagon, but the lower end was nothing but splinters.

The lid popped off and there was the body, all dressed in white, just as Mr. Stambo promised, even to a peaked angel's hood. It teetered forward and came sort of wafting out of the coffin box. It's feet touched the slab-rock, and then as we all watched pop-eyed it took off at an angle across the side of Snake Mountain, going like a shot-at cat, yellin "Wahoo, wa...hoo" like an Indian, and scattering chunks of yellow gumbo in all directions.

10 I never in my life saw anybody run as fast in yellow gumbo as whoever had been in that coffin box ran. Especially without num-hooks or ice-creepers. Cousin Manford and I, as well as a dozen or so of the younger men, tried to catch the corpse but we couldn't even keep it in sight. It reached the road, sailed over the rail fence, then over the hood of an automobile, and disappeared between the lines of cars parked on each side of the road, splashing windshields right and left, heading in the direction of Sny Magrew.

When I saw there was no use trying to catch the ghostly figure on foot I angled back toward the open gate to the road leading up to the cemetery, intending to get in my car and run the fugitive down and see who it was. I hadn't reached the fence yet when a new blue Cadillac came tearing down the road, nosed into the gateway to turn around, and spun its wheels getting underway again in the direction the corpse had taken. Evidently the driver had met the body on the road and had the same idea I had.

I wasn't close enough to recognize the motorist, except to see it was a man, but Shawn was in the seat beside him. Just as the car was turning around she recognized me and rolled the window down. "Hey, Boley," she yelled, "see you tonight at home."

Meanwhile, up around the wagon there was quite a lot of excitement. People milled about, examining the coffin box, talking and waving their arms. Several women had fainted, and when I got up there some of them were still lying in the mud. Aunt Maud was draped over a spring-seat, and Aunt Millie was stretched out in the bottom of the wagon. Mom was in her glory, working with handkerchiefs and camphor on all the patients. Uncle Parley Dooks had passed out, but Tom Larkey was reviving him by merely unfastening the tarpaulin and pulling it to one side so the rain could splash in his face.

Cousin Bonnie had, as Charles put it: "Collapsed." She had sat down squarely in the mud. Aunt Prue should have been alive to see the deep impression Bonnie was making. Charles was bent over her, slapping her wrists.

"What happened, Bolander?" he asked.

"I don't know what all happened," I said, "but I know one thing for sure."

I came right out and talked highbehind talk:

"*Aunt Prue has been carried by!*"

"One other fact is equally obvious," Charles said. "The funeral will not be held today."

Uncle LankyFrank came over to where Charles and I were and said, "You know sompn, Boley, I think that feller was Simon-Called-Peter Albans. Run like him."

Simon-Called-Peter Albans was the son of Tripoli Albans, the Turtle Holler Methodist part-time preacher. Simey was the one whom Aunt Prue bested in the Limber Jim and Shangle contest at Shake-Rag schoolhouse when she was seventy and he was seventeen, and double-jointed to boot. Simey was as near being considered "lackin'" as a Spunky Ridge residenter could get and not be. He was supposed to have studied the Books Of Moses. Some said he could make tables move mysteriously. Also he could predict weather. He had six toes on each foot, with webs between them, and he could swim the Saganois River easily. He could run like a hound dog for hours, and often did. Sometimes he ran off into the woods and lived for two or three days, but when he returned home he always brought a possum or a coon to eat.

I had heard about Simon-Called-Peter Albans, of course, from Mom, but I had never seen him. He was around thirty years old. Mom had said he was married to Placelia Watson, and that there was "nothin' pus-gutted about him."

"Could have been," I said, "but how could he have been away out there in Oregon?"

"Shucks," Uncle LankyFrank said, "the way he was a-goin' while ago it wouldn't take him *very* long to get anyplace."

"What does Simey do — work at — that he could have got in a box like that?"

"He's a cat-skinner," said Uncle LankyFrank.

"Did you hear the baggageman say anything while we were unloading Aunt Prue at Spunky Ridge?" I asked everybody.

Cousin Manford spoke up and said, "He mentioned somepn about eggs and mules, but I didn't get all of it, it was rainin' so hard."

"For the life of me, I can't figure it out," I said. "You saw us unload the coffin box. The Spunky Ridge platform is on the left side, going north, and we set the box on the left side of the car so it would be handy to unload. You helped unload it, too, Frank. Wasn't it in the same place?"

"Shore was. But some way or other Prue got out of it and this feller got in. Shorely he didn't come all the way from Or'gon in that box. Nothin' to eat, or no way for him to — thataway and that."

Already it was beginning to get dark. I began to feel creepy, for ghosts have been seen on Snake Mountain on rainy nights. I said hollowly, "Let's take a good look at that box."

"The thing that worries me," Uncle LankyFrank said — although anyone could see he wasn't worried too much — "is where Prue is at now. Nobody could ever keep track of her when she was alive, but now that she's dead it ort to be easier."

Tom Larkey was examing the coffin box when we got over to where it still stood leaning against the broken endgate. He said, "Oh-oh, b'Desus, looky here."

On the end of the box that still held together were several dents in the shape of small horseshoes. The toes on all of them pointed downward.

Only then did I remember the tricky triple valve on The Folly. The thought made me scringe.

"I'm not sure," I said slowly, "but I think I know about what happened: the triple valve stuck. I'll go back to Windfall tonight and talk to the train crew and find out for sure."

Mom was still out in the rain with her big black parasol, working first on one patient and then another, like a modern Florence Nightingale. When they had all recovered sufficiently to stand up by themselves we held a conference to decide what should be done, now that this new weary had come up.

"We won't have time any more today for the funeral — that's a cinch," I said, "so we may as well plan how we are going to work it tomorrow."

Aunt Maud was still feeling faint, and the protest

we all expected from her was feeble. "Can't Mr. Parker drive up to where sister Prue is at and bring her back? She must be up north there some place, thataway and that. Maybe at Vinton."

"But it's seventy-five or eighty miles up to Windfall, Aunt Maud," I said, "and we'd have to stop at every station and look for her. I don't think Lou Skates would put her off anymore—he'll carry her on into Windfall. Anyway, there's no point in driving that big hearse up there and back when we can wait till tomorrow and ship Aunt Prue back down on The Folly."

"I think that would be best," Mr. Parker said solemnly; and Aunt Maud didn't say any more, especially after Uncle Parley whispered to her that such an arrangement would give Bonnie a little more time to work on the obit.

"There is no reason to return the floral offerings to Saganois," Mr. Parker said. "There is plenty of moisture in the air to keep them fresh. They can be carried up and laid under the tent."

While we were putting the finishing touches on our plans for the next day, Latrum Squall, having overcome his fear of anything connected with a funeral, came mudding it up the hill. "Mr. Paydoley," he said, "Ah unhooked a fish for Mrs. Persnosky one time down in Yorkynut Slough, thought she might remember it." His eyes rolled warily at the broken coffin box. "Where she is?"

After I had explained everything to Latrum, he volunteered to help the pallbearers who had carried the grass and flower racks up to the tent the day before make another trip now with the flowers. Latrum reported everything all right up there—no water in the grave or anything—but he said the hard and steady rain was bringing out more and more of the picture of the lady on the tent, and more reading. "I kin make out two red spots inside the loop of beads," Latrum said. "There's a name showin', too, but it ain't hern."

"What is it?"

"Iola," Latrum said.

It was another weary, all right, but a minor one; and also one we couldn't do anything about — we certainly couldn't strike the tent and let the grave fill up with water. Besides, rain in an open grave is a sign that somebody in the family will pass away some time in the next year.

I shrugged Latrum's report off and said to the rest of them, "The Folly gets to Spunky Ridge from the north at ten oclock in the morning. If we could work it as we did today we could be all done by noon."

"That is," worried Mom, "if the same thing don't happen again, thataway and that."

"It won't," I said. "I'll see to that myself. Maybe this is a good thing to have happen, after all. Maybe now we will be able to read the same copy of the will that Aunt Prue intended us to read."

"I'll take Mollie and Charles and Bonnie back with me if you and Rembrandt want to go on to Windfall," Uncle LankyFrank offered.

"O.K.," I said. "We'll leave right away then. I'll have quite a few things to check on up there. I'll call Mom tonight and let you know what I find out. And, Tom, could you put in a new endgate?"

Tom said he sure could and sure would.

I had a last word with Mr. Parker. "Will the corpse be all right, Gib, or should I have an undertaker up at Windfall look at it?"

"I don't think that will be necessary," Parker said. "The modern techniques are very efficient."

I told him in a little more detail what I thought had happened, and finished with, "She might have been jounced around a good deal."

"You might have Mr. Jones look at the corpse, if it's convenient," Mr. Parker said.

I looked around for Rembrandt and couldn't find her. In fact, I hadn't seen her since the corpse took off across the mountain. I knew she hadn't fainted because I looked at all the fainted ones when I first came up from the gate and she wasn't among them.

"Do you know where Rembrandt is?" I asked Mom.

"Oh, she went back to the car as soon as the endgate broke," Mom said. "You wouldn't catch her out in all this rain.

Brandy was in the car, all right, listening to the radio. She was serene and relaxed, and looked as though she was ready to step out on a clothes-model's dais. All the other women who had followed the wagon were slopped up and frowsy, and not Brandy. I don't undestand how she does it. "Now do you believe Aunt Prue was a witch?" she asked me.

I got in, started the engine, and drove toward Windfall. "If Aunt Prue stepped out of one of those fence posts and flagged me down I'd stop and pick her up and not think there was anything unusual about it."

"Do you have any idea how it happened?"

"I think so. Partly, anyway: The coffin box was set on these rollers, like they always are, and when the triple valve stuck, the brakes grabbed. The triple valve controls the brakes—they're air brakes, you know—Westinghouse; and they've been about half-haywire for quite a while. We put wedges under the rollers to steady them, but probably they didn't hold. So when the brakes grabbed, the box probably rolled either forward or backward, depending on which way the train was going. It might have happened when Highspeed was backing up the stub track into Limberswitch, or it could have happened on Happy Rock hill.

"The end of the box could have slid against Chiquita's heels, or else Lupe's. Of course they didn't like that so they humped up, set their heels against the end of the box and sent it back the other way. A mule has a natural tendency to kick, and once started sometimes it's hard to make them stop. Anyway, that would account for the hoof-prints on the end of this other box.

"With that heavy coffin box sliding around on the floor, or it could have stayed on the rollers, it probably smashed into the egg crates and milk cans and stuff. That would account for the egg stains on this other box when we unloaded it. Something must have upset Lou Skates — knocked him down, I mean — because his overall looked like he had been sliding around on the floor along with everything else."

Brandy wouldn't believe my story. "I've heard you tell some tall hillbilly yarns," she said, "but nothing like that."

"I'm not exaggerating. It could easily have happened that way. You don't know how powerful a force momentum is on a train. Ever notice how you have to pull yourself along, or hold yourself back, when you try to walk up the aisle of a passenger coach when the train is speeding up or slowing down, either one? You've never ridden The Folly. Going around sharp curves I've been held against the side of the car lots of times — held there and couldn't move till we straightened out again. Highbehinds knew about G-Force long before the scientists did!"

"Even if such a thing did happen it doesn't explain the other box. You said there was just the one box in the car when the train left Saganois."

"That's right. That's an entirely different mystery. That smells to me like a typical Spunky Ridge trick — jest, as Charles would say. No vault, nothing but a guy in a box that looked like a coffin box. Somebody had even tacked the lid on—not very tight, only two or three nails in it. Anybody could have pushed their way out of it."

"Maybe whoever was in it was drunk."

"He didn't run like he was drunk, but he hollered like he was. He might have been drunk when he was put in—say, I just happened to think: I smelled Chinkapin Island whisky, but I figured it was them dam' horses. Ever' time they started, all the way. By Golly, I'll bet it was some of those Sny Magrew boys; Rollie Morgan and Eli Bates and Charlie Spoon. That bunch is pretty rough. River rats."

"I wonder what happed to Shawn, that she couldn't get here."

"Shawn! Didn't you see her?"

"No. Did you?"

"Did you see that blue Cadillac that turned around and chased the corpse?"

"Yes, but I was up by the wagon. I was too far away to tell who was in it."

"Shawn was in it."

"Then they're engaged! Bill sold all those hogs and bought a new Cadillac. I'll just bet they're engaged!" There were big-wedding plans in Rembrandt's excited voice.

"Talk about jumping to conclusions about the triple valve and the mules, you're worse than I am. It was Bill, all right, but I'll bet a cookie it was Bill Dugan; and I have a hunch he knew who the corpse was."

"Dugan?" Rembrandt whimpered. "You mean to say Shawn's mixed up with that rough Sny Magrew bunch? River rats?"

"Now, now, don't worry. Shawn's all right. She'll be home tonight, probably by the time we get there."

"Did she say that? Did you talk to her? What did she say?"

"We didn't have time to carry on a lengthy conversation. She said 'See you tonight at home.'"

11 Although it was still raining hard, when Rembrandt and I had eased our way along the little-used road from the cemetery out to the pavement, I hooked our old car up to forty-five and held it there. The traffic was light and we made good time. When we pulled up in front of the depot at Windfall, The Folly had just arrived and was unloading. Rembrandt went straight to a phone booth to call out home to see if Shawn was there.

On the station platform I met Steve Medill, the mail-transfer clerk, on his way back to his office from signing for the registers Substitute Scott had brought in. Steve worked a split shift: Four hours around six in the morning, and four around six at night. Scott had left for home, so I couldn't talk to him, much as I would have liked to, but Steve said sympathetically, "Had a little trouble, huh, Boley?"

"Ever hear of such a thing: Carrying a corpse by?"

"Too bad. Did the flowers get there all right?"

"O.K. Tell everybody thanks. Yeah, they're up there by the grave on top of Snake Mountain. We had everything to hold a funeral with except the corpse. I guess it's still over there in the baggage car unless Skates put it off somewhere between Spunky Ridge and here."

"It's there. Are you going to leave it in the baggage room overnight or take it to an undertaker?"

"Leave it in the baggage room. The undertaker at Saganois said it would be all right. You might tell the night crew to keep an eye on it — don't take a nap on it or anything."

"What all happened, anyway?"

"Don't know exactly until I talk to the train crew."

"That baggage car is in a devil of a mess. Looks like everything spilled in it."

"All I'm absolutely sure of is the coffin box was carried by. It was about halfway my fault. If it hadn't been raining so hard, and everybody so anxious to get back inside their cars, I would have noticed the box we unloaded was too light to have a steel vault in it. You see, there was only the one box in the car at Saganois, but there were two at Spunky Ridge. Lou picked one up somewhere."

"He says he didn't."

"He sure as the devil did. One looked the same as the other. That's why we got them mixed up."

"Well, things like that happen in the best regulated families, you know," Steve said inanely. "I got to be going. The boss is down here making an inspection." He slapped the pistol on his hip. "Even have to wear my gun."

"What I wanted to see you about: There's an airmail special-delivery register from Pistol River, Oregon addressed to me in care of Parker's Funeral Home in Sagnois somewhere between Oregon and here. Keep a lookout for it, will you?"

"Will do."

"I'll see you around four oclock tomorrow morning, before I start back down there. I'll have to leave before The Folly does in order to get down to Spunky Ridge and have things ready when the train gets there. The corpse will go back down on The Folly, of course."

Over at The Folly, old man Skates was standing in

the door of the baggage compartment. He had found his conductor's cap and was wearing it. It was smeared with white and yellow stains, but the CONDUCTOR on its brass plate could still be recognized. One lens of his glasses was gone and he peered at me apprehensively out of his one seeing eye. "I'm sorry, Boley," he said, "that I carried by the corpse, but it was just one of them things. Durn railroad company puts in Central Traffic Control and runs a train with only two men as long as it's on the main line, and they don't give a hoot how hard a man has to work out on a branch line."

"How in the world did it happen?"

"Well, at Sny Magrew I had three school-teachers get on. The station agent was sick and had went home, and I had to make change and everything. That's the hell of it, when one man has to run a train by hisself, I didn't see anybody load anything in the baggage car, I was back in the passenger section makin' out tickets and punchin' 'em and doin' all my other work.

"They was a bunch of young fellers hangin' around the depot, drunk and raisin' the devil, and this box was settin' on the platform. Hell, it's been there a week! Some sawmill man had a heavy drive shaft shipped in it. It must have weighed a thousand pounds. Took five of us to unload it—even Joe Moller got down out of the mail car and helped us. This guy—Dugan, his name is—unpacked it and left the box on the platform. I remember he loaded it on a low-boy trailer hooked behind a big loggin' truck."

"I see. Dugan, huh? Is that the name of the guy who bought that 1500 acres of timber along the river below Sny Magrew?"

"That's him. He's got a saw-mill down there a block long. Just settin' it up. Hell, he's got fifteen or twenty men cuttin' timber. You can see 'em from the tracks. I'll bet that feller's got a dozen trucks and caterpillars and low-boys workin' down there."

"Where's he from, anyway?"

"Some place over in Missouri, Wild Ike told me. Musta knowed Truman. He's only about thirty, and I bet that feller makes money hand over fist."

I was glad to learn more about Mr. Dugan, seeing as how it was obvious Shawn had not taken Summer Street home last Tuesday morning, but right now I wanted to find out more about what had happened to The Folly coming up. I pulled old man Skates back on the subject.

"Somebody loaded this box that was on the platform into the baggage car then, when you weren't looking?"

Lou folded down to a squat in the doorway. "I guess they did," he said aplogetically. "No other way it could have got there. I been thinkin' about it ever' since it happened, and I'll just bet one of this bunch of hellions was drunk, so the rest of them put him in this box and loaded him onto the train, just for a joke."

"I noticed there wasn't even a way-bill on it."

"There wasn't anything. If it hadn't a been the same size and shape as the coffin box I wouldn't a carried by the corpse. And if it hadn't a been for that Gawd-dam' trickle valve the boxes wouldn't a got mixed up."

"So the valve went bad again?"

"Oh, that gawd-dam' trickle valve! Ike began to have trouble with it as soon as we left Saganois. It was worse than last Tuesday when you was on."

Highspeed Skaderight, having turned out all lights, shut off all gadgets and otherwise prepared The Folly for the night, climbed down from the cab and joined us. "If you think that trickle valve was actin' up last Tuesday you ort to have been along today," he said heartily. "I thought I was goin' to stand her on her head a time or two."

Wild Ike Highspeed was proud of his title. On The Folly he was the glory man, sat in the cat-bird seat, drew two days pay for one of work, and anything that happened to his august person was of utmost importance not only to himself, but should be to everyone else.

"I first noticed it comin' down Happy Rock hill, this side of Rabbit College. That was the first time she grabbed."

"That was when the coffin box broke loose and come rollin' into the egg crates," old man Skates said. "Smashed two of them all to hell and knocked my lunch all over ever'thing. Even knocked me out of my armchair and hurt my knee." He fixed me with his one good eye:

"Them ain't my egg stains on the box. I et off my chest!"

"She stuck tight for a second," Wild Ike boasted, "then let loose all at once. She bucked like a bronco: 'Wild Ike Highspeed Skaderight on Folly, out of Chute Five.' I stayed on top of her, though, because I'm the guy that can stay on top of anything the Come Back & Quick puts under me — and bring her in on the second, too, or maybe ahead of time. But if my seat hadn't had a back on it, or if I didn't have good cord-nation I'd a landed on the dynamo!"

"That was when the coffin box rolled back the other way, into Lupe," Skates said. "I don't know whether it's a good idy or not to set them coffin boxes on rollers — ort to use blocks. When Lupe looked around and saw that thing comin' at her, she humped up and set both heels against the end of it and kicked. And here it come back again and broke the rest of the egg crates open — and you ort to a seen the milk splatterin'. Look at that mess!" He pointed at the floor, which was covered with a slick mixture of milk and eggs. "Hell, look at me!"

Skates changed the balance point of his squat in the baggage-car door and squinted down at me. "I dodged it that time, though. I just wretched up and grabbed the safety bar and pulled myself up out of the way. Even then, Chiquita kicked my glasses off and broke one side—I never saw such mules to kick in all my life. If it wasn't one it was the other, trying to keep that coffin box away from them. I thought they never would stop."

Skaderight's heavy lips flapped. "The next time that little ol' trickle valve went haywire was comin' down Jerry hill. That time it was worse than ever. We stopped dead. I had to get out and hit it with my hammer to break it loose."

"I think that was the time the boxes got mixed up," Mr. Skates explained, "with this other box next to the door and yours toward the middle. Both of them was slidin' around by that time, on account of the floor bein' so slick, and they could a changed places without me a-knowin' it, as busy as a man is on this run where he has to punch tickets, throw switches, handle baggage and express and do a lot of other jobs. I'm sorry, Boley, that it happened, but it was just one of them things."

"That's all right, Lou," I said. "It wasn't altogether your fault."

The old fellow looked relieved, and asked, "You didn't bury that other box, did you?"

"No," I said. "Your guess was right about a guy being in it. But he jumped out and took off. Scared all of us half to death."

"I kept pullin' the signal cord to let Ike know there was somepn wrong with the brakes, but it didn't seem to do any good. I could hear the whistle up in the cab, too." Skates one-eyed Wild Ike accusingly.

"'I don't give a hoot for your silly little toot,'" Wild

Ike chanted. "Saw that on the back of a car the other day, thought it was pretty good. Hell, Skates, I knew there was somepn wrong. You didn't have to signal me."

A train inspector came along past The Folly, tapping its wheels with his hammer. Wild Ike collared him, shook a grimy, admonishing finger under his nose:

"If you don't put a new trickle valve on The Folly tonight, or take that'n off and grind it, I won't take her out tomorrow. Just don't bother to call me, I won't do it. I've put that trickle valve on my work sheet ever' night for a month, but you guys sit around on your single-o's all night and don't do a dam' thing. Now see what you've done: You've made us carry a lady's corpse by!" He strutted away, a pompus cock of rolling stock, toward the taxicab stands.

"One good thing," I said to Mr. Skates. "Nobody was hurt. We can send the corpse back down to Spunky Ridge with you in the morning and have the funeral when it gets there."

"I'll make sure it gets off tomorrow. And I'll have the boys nail some cleats on the drain boards to hold it in place."

The depot boys unloaded Aunt Prue and wheeled her carefully across the platform and into the big baggage room. I saw Brandy looking out the depot window and went over to her. "That's what happened, all right—about the triple valve. I'll call Mr. Jones and then we can eat supper here in the depot while he's on his way down. Did you talk to Shawn?"

Brandy shook her head. "Nobody answered. It's been fifteen minutes since I called. I'll try again."

While Rembrandt called out home, I saved a dime by calling Mr. Jones from the Transfer Office. No answer—it was seven oclock by this time—so I called his home.

"Hello," he said.

I didn't know him any too well. I had shot skeet and trap with him a few times at the gun club; and I had given him a few postmarks of places like Jones, Oklahoma; Diggs, Virginia; and Graves, Georgia, just to give him an idea of how to start his collection. Locally he was quite well known as a collector, specializing in stamps, coins and epitaphs, but had a good display of salt and pepper shakers, too, as well as a few interesting postmark sentences. An alert, quiet, bright-eyed little chap about my age, he was good at ping-pong.

"Hello, Mr. Jones," I said, "this is Boley Paydoley, down at the depot. My aunt died."

I went on to tell him my story, and he said he would be glad to come down and take a look at the corpse as soon as he ate his supper.

We needn't, however, have gone to any such trouble. For when Mr. Jones raised the lid of the coffing, there was Aunt Prue, dressed white, with a white hood to hold her hair in place, looking as natural as could be, and just as I remembered her.

She wore a faint mischievous grin, as though she had in mind some new trick to devil us. I actually believe that Aunt Prue had lived life in such great gulps, and with such zest, that although her body had worn out, her frolicking spirit carried on for awhile.

When I got back inside the depot Rembrandt was sitting on edge on the edge of one of the long benches.

"Everything's all right," I said. "Let's go home."

"I talked to Shawn. They just got home. She said to hurry and get out there. Said she had a surprise for us."

"Hog-man Bill or Saw-mill Bill?"

"She didn't say. Oh, Boley, I'm afraid it's Dugan! And she hasn't known him long enough—just since Tuesday. What if they're engaged? Or maybe married! River rat!"

12 A new blue mud-splattered Cadillac was parked in the yard when Brandy and I got home. Bill Dugan and Shawn were munching popcorn at the kitchen table when we came through the back door, after putting the car away.

"Mother, this is Bill Dugan," Shawn jumped up and said. She nodded at me. "You two have already met. We're going to be married." She showed her left hand, on which a modest diamond ring gleamed.

"How do you do, Mrs. Paydoley," Dugan said. He nodded at me, but it was plain that Brandy was his No. 1 target. He would have taken a step toward her if she had given him any sign of welcome, and taken her hand if she would have offered it, I guess, the way he had scrambled to his feet when we appeared. Brandy, however, just stood there giving him the twice-over and then some more, first flicking a subconscious glance at his midriff, as any normal woman does when she meets a man for the first time, but spending most of her attention on his face. Her arm was around Shawn's shoulder, and she was unsmiling when she said, "How do you do?"

From dark, bristly crew-cut to square-toed shoes Rembrandt studied Bill Dugan. His short-sleeved blue chambray shirt was open at the neck, its tail tucked neatly into his gray trousers. His arms were almost as big as my legs. He was an even six feet tall, I learned later, but his thick body did not make him seem that tall. It was his eyes that I remember so well as he stood there. They were steel gray, and a little stern, unblinking as they met Rembrandt's critical stare.

They stood eyeing each other a few seconds, then a mischievous look appeared on Dugan's face as he snapped to attention and turned slowly around. When he had completed the circle and was again facing Rembrandt he walked over and knelt in front of her, took her right hand and raised it to his lips.

"Thank you, Mrs. Paydoley," he said, "for bringing up a daughter like Shawn. I've been looking for a girl like her for a long time. I love her. I'm going to marry her."

He got up, took a step backward and folded his enormous arms. "In you I see Shawn when she is as old as you are, and I'm more than satisifed. Thank you again. You have helped make me the happiest man in the world."

Brandy's defenses crumpled. She left Shawn and went to Dugan. Her head found his shoulder, and he stood there smoothing her graying hair and winking over the top of her head at Shawn and me.

The ice was broken and the atmosphere became pleasantly warm. While Rembrandt and Shawn chattered in the kitchen, Mr. Dugan and I went upstairs to my den. Although it didn't make any difference one way or another to me whom Shawn married—I holding the opinion that parents shouldn't interfere with their children's choices of spouses, after having done their best to educate them and make good citizens of them—I wanted to give this guy the postmark test.

Dugan wanted to talk to me, too. "Too bad about today, Boley," he said. "I guess I can call you Boley. Shawn does."

"Go ahead."

"It was one of my men—fellow named Albans—that caused all the trouble. I'm sorry. I feel responsible."

So Uncle LankyFrank was right about the fast runner being Simon-Called-Peter Albans, the Turtle

Holler part-time preacher's son. Frank had seen Simey running through the woods or on the roads lots of times.

"You aren't, you know," I said. "But how did he do it?"

"Got drunk; and some of the other boys put him in that box and threw it on the train. Guess they thought that would sober him up as quick as anything else. Some of my boys are pretty rough. Most of them live down around Sny Magrew and Limberswitch. They're not bad, just a little wild. I don't have any trouble with them, except to straighten them out once in a while. They loaded up on Chinkapin Island whiskey," the young man said. "Made on the island and bottled behind a stump. You can even taste the willows in it."

Dugan grinned – I watched his face wrinkle, finding a bit out more about what kind of a guy he was. So far, there existed no noticeable rapport between us. I asked carefully, "Did you fire Albans?"

"No. The gang has an excuse to play around. They haven't been able to work since Wednesday – all this rain. You'll hold the funeral tomorrow, I suppose."

"As soon as the train gets to Spunky Ridge – around ten oclock. The hearse will meet it there, the same as it did today."

"I'll have some cats and low-boys at the foot of the hill tomorrow when the hearse gets there. You won't have to bother with the wagon."

He spoke calmly, and as though he had organized his thoughts ahead of time and knew exactly what he was going to say. Tonight he was all business, but I knew he could be frivolous because I had heard Shawn and him fling the persiflage about, the morning he had ridden with us. I began to like the guy. We sat in front of my old desk, smoking cigarettes and using the same ash tray.

"You don't have to do that." I said.

"I want to, Boley. I'll have tarps on the low-boys so the older folks can ride up in the dry. I can even pull the hearse up with a cat. Might look a little better." He gave me a searching look. "It would be a big favor to me."

I nodded dumbly. The guy was irrestible. "O.K."

"By the way, who owns the Dinnegan cemetery?"

"It belongs to all the descendants of the first Dinnegan — Hugh, his name was — who settled here in 1825. It can never be sold. President Monroe signed the title to that land."

I went on to tell him about the concrete statues of Grandpa and Grandma Dinnegan that sat on one corner of the triangular graveyard, and how the graves of their descendants were planned to fan out behind theirs, one generation after the other. "There's forty acres in all, but only two or three in the cemetery proper. Nobody but Dinnegan relatives are buried there."

"Who takes care of it?"

"Nobody much. I guess the Barnes brothers as much as anybody. They've dug all the graves there for the last forty years, anyway. Their mother was a Dinnegan, and they just took on the job voluntarily. There's supposed to be a meeting of all the relatives every year at the cemetery on the Fourth Of July — kind of a family reunion, but nobody ever goes any more. I used to go when I was a kid. Nice place for a picnic back of it, in the woods along Rocky Branch. There's been talk of starting the picnics again but we never have. People are too busy — too concerned with their own private affairs — to do anything like that any more."

I was as bad as Mom, yapping about the Dinnegans — a regular blabbermouth. I lit another cigarette and decided to slow down or Dugan might think I was windy.

"When I marry Shawn will I be eligible to be buried there?"

"Sure." I wondered what he had in mind. Surely he wasn't thinking about passing away yet. "Of course. Why?"

"I'd like to build a good road up Snake Mountain. I have some grading equipment—cats and bulldozers and scrapers, that I got hold of last winter. I'd like to experiment on a road like that before I bid on any county or state road jobs, just to prove I could do the work. I'd donate everything, of course."

I thought Gee Whiz! this guy talks about road-building machinery like I talk about rifles and shotguns. Caterpillar tractors and bulldozers cost fifteen or twenty thousand dollars apiece; and the scoops and scrapers used to build roads nowadays haul fifteen cubic yards of dirt at a time and are almost as expensive as the tractors.

I wondered what the relatives would say about Dugan building such a road. The subject had been mentioned many times in the past, but nothing had ever been done about it. A road up rock-jutting Snake Mountain would cost a lot of money, and none of the Dinnegans except Aunt Prue had ever made much more money than it took to support them. They had even talked about doing it with the money they expected Aunt Prue to leave them, if there was enough left after Mom had put a new roof on her house, Aunt Millie had bought herself a monument, Aunt Maud had bought Cousin Manford a new compressor for his deep freeze, and Uncle LankyFrank had installed a water system in his farmhouse, now that he already had a television set.

"I don't think anybody would object," I said, "but we'd have to handle the idea with kid gloves. Those hillbillies down there are proud — sensitive about anything like that.

"I know. I'm a hillbilly myself."

"That right?"

"From Missouri. Down around Marshfield."

"I know where it is. St. Louis & Oklahoma City R.P.O."

"R.P.O.?"

"Railway Post Office. Frisco line. In the Postal Transportation Service all rail lines are designated by the towns between which they operate." I sounded stiff. I had tried to inject some dignity and importance into my statements, but I have a devil of a time talking importantly and with dignity.

"I see," Dugan said. He didn't say it contemptuously, as many people do when speaking of anything concerned with the Post Office Department, the employes of which are considered by some to be as near slaves as it is possible for Americans to become.

It wasn't much of a job — that of transporting the United States mails — compared to the important work young Bill Dugan, who was but half my age, had done and was planning to do. Poking letters and slinging newspapers and parcels about do not compare very favorably to sawing lumber and railroad ties, and building roads. I felt a little icky trying to pump a measure of prestige into my work. However, a man likes to justify his job, and I was aware that no matter how far down the social or economic scale an American slides, if he has any kind of address at all, the United States Post Office Department has a line on him — cares about him — sort of like God. His letter might well travel to its destination in the same package containing the president's letter.

"It's not much of a job," I said, "but it's the only one I ever had. It's the only job I know of that women have never held. No woman has ever been assigned to a Railway Post Office." I was going to add the ancient highbehind gag that it was because they didn't have a bag to carry the mail in, but thought I better hadn't. "I've been at it forty-three years."

"I had an uncle in the Railway Mail Service. Ran between St. Louis and Little Rock. Iron Mountain road. He used to play with those little white cards—had a case he poked them in when he was preparing to take an examination. I guess you know."

"Yeah, I know."

One thing I have noticed about the Railway Mail Service—or Postal Transportation Service, as it is known now—never yet have I met anyone who didn't have a relative or an acquaintance working in it, and the fact is always mentioned. To people outside the service there is something romantic and glamorous and exciting about transporting United States mail across the country, distributing it on the way. The work is different—more free, and independent of petty, carping supervision—than that performed in post offices, where clerks, except the ladies when they are in their toilets, are even subjected to the indignity of being spied on by inspectors slew-footing the galleries built especially for the purpose.

Forty or fifty postmarks, separated to nouns, adjec-adjectives, verbs, etc., were spread out on my desk where I had been fooling with them Tuesday morning when the phone call came in from Oregon. I raked them together in neat piles and opened one of my albums. I usually trim my postmarks to about the size of an ordinary calling card, just so all the wavy lines and other characteristics of special cachets remain.

"Here's something you might be interested in, Bill," I said. "Kind of an odd hobby of mine. You can arrange them to say all sorts of things. Works a good deal like

Scrabble." I showed him some of my set-ups: Myrtle, Idaho; Given, West Virginia; Fifty-six, Arkansas; Bowlegs, Oklahoma; and one or two more. "Why don't you fix up a sentence? I'll go downstairs and see if I can find something to drink."

Brandy and Shawn were still in the kitchen, talking a blue streak.

"How are you two getting along up there?" Brandy asked. Already she was in the role, of the beaming, scheming, dreaming mother-in-law. For Shawn had completely sold her on the ridiculous cliche of acquiring a son instead of losing a daughter.

"All right. He's quite a guy. Hairy, huh, Shawn?"

"Whiskers to his eyes!" Shawn said. Her eyes shone, and her left one was noticeably bigger, like it gets when she is in a duck blind and meat is in the air.

I digged her — not for nothing have I helped bring up an atom-age daughter — and came back with "He counts down with you, doesn't he?"

"Ever since five o'clock last Tuesday morning. And to think how near I came to taking Summer Street home."

I gave her the test I consider the mostest. "How about clipping hair out of his ears or biting out turned-under whiskers?"

"I used to see Mom do that to you and thought it was awful. But I tried it on Bill Dugan — and oooh!" She shivered ecstatically.

"Suppose he wants to take off for South America or Alaska or some place like that with his saw mill?"

"I'd go — anywhere — with him."

She stood, young and strong and ready for the work for which she was born. Bill Dugan, the lumberman, knew a good tree when he saw one. And that's what she was, this beautiful daughter of mine. My thoughts flew back to 1918, just before I went into military uniform the first time. She who was Miss Rembrandt Foster was sitting on my lap in a big chair in the Foster parlor. The expression "over the top" was heard often in those days, because that was what so many of our soldiers were doing in the trench fighting of World War I. I, too, knew what I wanted. I asked Miss Rembrandt Foster, "Will you go...over the top...with me?" Her answer had been the same as Shawn's a moment ago: "I'd go—anywhere—with you."

I looked at Shawn standing there by the kitchen table. She was Brandy Foster, in 1918. She wore the same rapt look, had the same shine in her eyes.

"But, Shawn," Rembrandt said. "Are you sure you want to marry him? Knowing him such a short time? Remember, he's going to be the father of your children."

"I know it," Shawn said. "That's why I'm so anxious to get him working at the job!"

Headlights flashed in through the kitchen window and a demanding clarion horn blasted out as a car stopped in the drive at the side of the house.

"That's old Tar," Shawn said, "the Balkan with the Balkan ideas about women. I'm supposed to jump up and run to him, fluttering my eyes. Well, I'm a little Balky myself—but I'll go out and talk to him. Give that Irishman upstairs something to do—play with your postmarks or something—until I can get rid of my other Bill."

Women are cruel and ruthless, I have learned, once they make up their odd minds and decide what they want. I hoped Shawn would use her bludgeon mercifully. I liked Bill Tarsevik. However, he could never have kept pace with Shawn, who had more ideas in a minute than he had in a month. He perhaps would have pulled up even with her eventually, but for many years he would have been like my Uncle Phineas Persnosky, who wore himself out trying to keep up with Aunt Prue.

Rembrandt and I were left looking at each other. In our more than forty years of marriage we have faced a good many crises together. I went over and kissed her, just to show her I was pulling along with her through this one. "Things happening fast, huh, kid?"

She looked at me as though I had busted out with a boop-a-doop in the midst of *God Save The King*.

13 I got a bottle of my home-made elderberry wine and a couple of glasses and returned upstairs. Mr. Dugan was at my desk. He turned his back to it and nudged the chair I had been sitting on toward a card table with his foot, then leaned back against the desk. I couldn't see what he had done, if anything, with my postmarks.

"How long have you been in the postal service?" He picked up his glass of wine and took a sip, relished it, and said, "Good."

"Since 1919. It's the only job I ever had except when I was in the army."

"Could you retire?"

"I could, but I figured I'd stay in till I'm seventy — or at least sixty-five."

"Do you think your run will stay on that long?"

"I don't know. Rail lines are being discontinued all over the country. Competition from trucks and busses —that run on roads maintained by the public—and from subsidized air and inland-water routes, is just too much for them. There have been rumors that The Folly might quit any time, but so far the Burlington Route hasn't asked the Commerce Commission for a hearing to take her off. I'm keeping my fingers crossed."

I can get excited about the plight of the railroads. In the years since I had climbed into a mail car for the first time I had seen rail transportation reach its peak and then decline because of what I considered unfair competition. I had been a tiny part of a great industry that, although enjoying for years what practically amounted to a monopoly on transportation, did a good job at a reasonable price, built its own roads and maintained them, and more than did its part to build up the country. No other common carrier, in my opinion, is more worthy of modern come-to-papa Federal subsidy —but gets none. And no other form of public transportation is needed more than railroads.

I invited argument. "With labor unions tying one foot, the Commerce Commission tying the other, and Federal subsidies to competitors holding one hand, it's a wonder the railroads stumble along as well as they do."

Dugan listened attentively as I expounded at length on one of my favorite subjects for argument. He agreed that I had a point here and there. Then he changed the subject of conversation:

"You know a lot about guns, Shawn told me."

"A little. I've hunted all my life; and have several primer-poppers around the house."

Shawn said she had loaded my 30-06 and brought it upstairs when she stayed alone. I stepped across the hall into her room and got it. It is an army Springfield that I bought from the Rock Island arsenal in 1946 after I was discharged from the army and was still on terminal leave. I had converted it to a sporter: reshaped the stock to make a better grip, took off the bayonet lug and most of the wood off the forearm, and equipped it with a Weaver K-4 scope on a Pachmayr Lo-Swing mount. It was a nice, serviceable hunting rifle. I'd killed five deer, three elk, a bear and a moose with it.

Dugan took the gun and the first thing he did was rack the bolt back to see if it was loaded. I liked that. It showed he knew something about guns and was a potential hunter—if not a real one—even though he might be a yayhoo hunter who killed only blue-rocks or bulls-eyes; for all guns are loaded until you look at them yourself and find out for certain whether they are or not. Dugan didn't strike me as being a guy who would forget his ammunition or get lost in the woods and yell "Yay...hoo" so somebody could find him.

He racked the magazine empty and the half-dozen cartridges clattered onto the floor. "We had all Garands in Korea," he said as he bent over to pick them up, "but you know what this model does year after year at Camp Perry. I still think the '03 is the best rifle ever built except maybe the Mauser. Did you remodel the stock yourself?"

I nodded. "Mounted the scope, too. I like to play around with stuff like that. I even have a rifle range below the house. You can get 125 yards if you back up into the brush."

He laid the rifle across his knees and looked up at me:

"How would you like to run a gun stock factory?"

I grunted. "Heck, I don't know anything about running a factory. All I know how to do is distribute mail. I wouldn't—"

Suddenly I remembered last Tuesday morning when he ran out of gas with his truck of walnut logs. He had said something about taking them to a gun-stock factory that had burned down and was starting up again.

"Whose factory?"

"Mine."

"The one that burned, out at the edge of town?"

He nodded. "I bought it right. I'm going to rebuild it and get it going again. I'd like for you to take full charge of it."

I thought: You big overbearing louse! You might be a big wheel and a shrewd operator that's used to getting his own way, but you can't pull a pawky Sandy McIntosh like that on me. I stood up.

"See here, Mr. Dugan, I may be only a raggety-rumped mail-car highbehind that makes five thousand a year while you make maybe twenty times that much, but I have some pride. I wouldn't run your goddam gun-stock factory on any terms, even if I could. You might have bought Shawn but you can't buy me!" I realized I was making a fool of myself but I was seeing red.

He jumped to his feet, mad as hell, and stood facing me:

"I didn't buy Shawn and you know it! You know as well as I do that she's the kind that all the money in the world couldn't buy. You didn't bring her up that way. And as for your goddam silly pride, it's your ridiculous, super-sensitive hillbilly blood that warps your judgment. Damn to hell, Boley, can't I offer you a job without you getting sore?"

When two men start swearing at each other over a business deal they forget about pretense and tact and diplomacy, and dig down under each other's hides and get at their true natures. We stood glaring at each other like a couple of tom-cats on the prod. Dugan's face was flushed, his eyes brilliant:

"Can I be blamed for making more money than you do? I cut the damned railroad ties that your mail car runs on. You see that mail orders for the ties are delivered to me. Your job helps me and my job helps you. One would be S.O.L. without the other. I can't help it if mine pays more money than yours."

I took a turn around the room, lit a cigarette. Dugan said, "I thought I was doing my future father-in-law a favor. I know how you feel about The Folly staying on, and I know how the Q feels about it. Lots of times I ship by rail when I could do better with trucks, just because I want the train to stay on at least until I can cut a patch of timber down there below Sny Magrew. I don't care about the passenger service but I sure want the way-freight to stay."

Our stairway has a landing halfway up, where it makes a right-angle turn, and through the open door of my den I saw the shadows of Shawn and Rembrandt's heads on the wall above the landing. They were listening shamelessly, facing each other, squared away, fists up, Rembrandt was me and Shawn was Dugan. I maneuvered to keep myself next to the door so Dugan couldn't see them.

"You know guns," he said. "I got a gun-stock factory. What is more logical than wanting you to run it?"

Shawn's footwork was excellent. Her fists protected her jaws. She jabbed with her left, then crossed a right.

"I couldn't do it, anyway," I said. "You'll have to get somebody else."

Rembrandt parried the blows, than launched an attack herself. Shawn retreated.

Dugan said, "I don't want anybody else, I want you. Look, Boley: I made some money on hogs last year and bought some road-building equipment. The year before that I had some extra cash and bought a thousand gilts—already bred. I rent these hogs around to farmers. They feed and take care of them, and I take one pig out of each litter when they get to marketing weight—around two hundred pounds. With two litters a year, I get four hundred pounds of meat a year out of each hog—and I still own the brood sows. One farmer out here west of town—Bill Tarsevik—has 103 of my hogs, and just the other day he sold their pigs. I took my share of the money and bought this gun-stock factory."

On the stairway wall I saw Rembrandt's flailing fists falter, then drop to her side. She was a hurt boxer, clinching with her opponent. Dugan kept talking:

"You see, Boley, the tax structure we have in this country *forces* a man to grow. I can't afford to make money and let it lay idle. I've got to expand—that's why I'm going to build some public roads. As a guard against recession, Congress voted two billion dollars to build roads. I'm going to start in the southern half of Starbuck County, which God knows needs some passable roads. Starbuck hasn't been spending its share of the gas-tax money on roads, and the other day the State Legislature got on them for letting it pile up. That's why I want to experiment on a road up Snake Mountain—if I can build one up there I can build one anywhere."

"Then you're just starting out in the road business?"

"Yes, and it gripes the hell out of me to hear a guy yell how hard it is to start a business; when he says the Government throws too many obstacles in his path, especially if he hires more than six or eight people. Of course there's a few regulations that could be considered obstacles—there wouldn't be much kick in making money if there weren't. But they're prods in the caboose as well as obstacles."

I felt weak, sat back down in my chair. To the devil with the feminie fisticuffs at the bottom of the stairway. Anyway, I thought they had stopped. Bill Dugan was an example of the "younger generation," about which so many people were worried. I wished everybody in America could have heard him spout off:

"I'd sure like to have you run the gun-stock factory, Boley," he coaxed. "I know you could do it."

I shook my head. Acceptance of his offer meant I would have to retire. Retirement, however, was several years away—if I was to draw the maximum annuity. I hadn't thought much about it except in a vague, desultory way. Hiding safely behind the protective skirts of a piddling Government job, I had become stale in my thinking.

My job meant security. It had carried me through the depression of the Dirty Thirties, even though my salary had been slashed to slivers. I owed it loyalty. I would stay till I was seventy. The idea was pleasing.

As a matter of cold fact, I didn't have the moral courage to rise from my scantily padded but secure Civil Service seat and engage in the aggressive competition of the business world, just as Aunt Prue had said years ago. However, I still stubbornly refused to admit that the accusation was altogether true.

"Can't do it, Bill," I said. "I'd have to retire."

"Sure you would, but would that be so tragic—start realizing on an investment you started in 1920? Look, Boley, how much would you draw if you retired now?"

"Around two-fifty a month."

"And how much if you stay till you're seventy?"

"Three hundred or so."

"All right; to make easy figuring, say you're sixty now. You'll draw thirty thousand dollars between now and the time you're seventy, all clear—it won't cost you anything except the income tax on it. How long are you going to have to live, *after you reach seventy*, to absorb thirty thousand dollars at fifty dollars a month? Why don't you start cashing in on that investment? You should have done it the day you became eligible to retire."

"I've thought about it," I said weakly, "but never seriously. A guy wants to work as long as he can and draw as much as he can. His income will be cut quite a bit, and with prices going up all the time."

Dugan begged me, "Don't be like so many other guys, Boley: Work at a job as rough as yours is till you go under, then kick off before you draw half a dozen annuity checks. Quit now, draw your pension, and run the factory. You can do it; you're the right man for it; you can even talk gun stocks to the Ordnance Department. There's another good reason: Suppose The Folly is taken off and you have to crowd into the organization of another rail line—make everybody junior to you in seniority sore; and you'd have to study a lot of new territory."

"I can't take the job, Bill. I'm sorry. I'm sorry about flying off the handle, too."

"That's all right, Boley," he said sadly. "At least it cleared the air. We know where we stand now. I'm sorry you can't see your way clear to taking the job."

He started downstairs, but stopped at the door and turned around:

"Shawn and I will be married Sunday, over in Missouri. I know a Justice of the Peace at Bowling Green."

The blow landed squarely on my heart. All through the years that I had watched Shawn grow into a beautiful woman I had looked forward to her wedding. She was a fine human being, a precious living part of Rembrandt and me, that we had created from our own bodies—from our deep abiding love for each other; that we had moulded to the pattern of our spiritual selves. Some day I would be proud to present her to the man she had chosen to marry.

I managed to stand up and face Dugan—and noticed the shadows on the wall again. They were absolutely motionless.

"This is quite a surprise, Bill, having the wedding so soon. I thought you might wait and be married in church. Rembrandt and I have always planned that Shawn would be married in church. She's the only daughter we have, and we looked forward to having a nice wedding for her. It would be like having our own wedding again—bring back a lot of memories. Rem and I didn't have much of a wedding, and no honeymoon at all. It was war time, thataway and that."

There was a hard ache in my throat, but I finished what I wanted to say:

"I guess it's no use asking you to imagine yourself in my place. Some day maybe you will be able to, and will...if you have a daughter. I think fathers look forward to giving their daughters away in marriage as the most important thing they have ever done in all their lives. It's the culmination of a worthy achievement, that they have struggled for...for a long time. I know it would be a proud moment for me."

I begged with my eyes, my voice, my entire being:

"You wouldn't wait and have the wedding in church, would you?"

There was a rippling of the muscles beneath the skin on Dugan's tightly clenched jaws. His gray eyes were rock hard. He said evenly:

"We'll be married in church if you take the job."

For a moment I couldn't speak. This was the ruthless pressure of the business world; this was IT. The chips were down, the ducks on the pond. I held out my hand and Dugan grasped it.

"O.K.," I said.

He let out a wild whoop, almost floored me with a slap on my back, and bounded down the stairs. I followed. Slowly.

Brandy was at the foot of the stairway. Her cheeks were flushed and her dark eyes shone as she stood recovering from Dugan's harvesting hug. She said gaily, "So you're going to retire at last?"

"How did you know?" I asked inanely, for I knew she and Shawn had been listening. I was still in more or less of a daze, I guess.

"I'm glad, Boley." She put her arms around my neck and kissed me, and I felt a lot better.

It is something of a shock to retire from a job a person has worked at for more than forty years. It is like moving into an entirely new world and taking up an entirely new life. I didn't know what to do first.

"Go ahead and call the Transfer Office," Brandy said happily. "Tell them you are going to retire, and aren't going to work any more. Tell them you're sick, and to keep the sub on your run indefinitely. Tell them anything!"

"I can't call now. It's nine oclock. Steve's gone home." I was like a kid.

"The other man—what's his name: Morrison—is there. Tell him, call the Anniston office, call everybody! Tell them Boley Paydoley on The Folly is going to retire! Going to get a *good* job and make something out of himself at last! Shout it from the housetops!"

I caught her spirit. "Going to maybe have a business with a thousand-dollar light bill every month!"

"I've been wanting you to retire ever since you

became eligible. Now go ahead! Celebrate!"

I went to the phone and called the Transfer Office. Harry Morrison, one of the night men, answered.

"This is Boley Paydoley," I said. "I'm going to retire. I'm sick. I'm not going to work any more. Tell Scotty to stay on my run."

The words sounded strange. It was hard to believe I was saying them.

"The Superintendent is here, Boley, making an inspection. I'll let you talk to him."

The chief of the Anniston District Office, Mr. George Gregory Mansfield, was a political appointee, although there is supposed to exist no such creature in the United States Postal Transportation Service, where theoretically all vacancies are filled by senior employes, provided they can pass the examinations. He was five or six years my junior in Civil Service. He preferred to be called Mr. Mansfield. When he answered I said:

"Hello, George, fix up my retirement papers when you get back to Anniston, and keep Scotty running for me until all my sick leave is used up—this is Boley Paydoley."

"Very well, Mr. Paydoley. I think that is an excellent idea. Because the Windfall & Saginois R.P.O. will be discontinued at the end of the fiscal year."

After what I'd just gone through nothing could surprise me. Besides, I had been expecting the little train to come off. "The Folly and I will retire together," I said. "I have enough sick leave to last about that long. I'm not going to work any more."

"You are ill, then?"

"Oh, yes, I've been ailing for some time now."

"What is the exact nature of your ailment?"

"I got a sore back."

I hung up and said, "Well, that's that, thataway and that. It's hard to believe."

Brandy was already making plans. "We should take a long vacation after the wedding," she suggested, "before you go to work at your new job. I won't know how to act, not having to get up at four oclock in the morning every other week."

"Maybe Aunt Prue will leave me the Cadillac and we can use it for our vacation."

"Don't plan on it. Get her buried first. She's probably planning more devilment right now."

"Things should work out all right tomorrow. Bill is going to haul everybody, dead or alive, up the hill — if you listened I don't have to tell you. And you listened because I saw you and Shawn fighting on the wall. How do you like this saw-mill Bill, anyway?"

"All right. I think Shawn has at last met her match. I don't think she has known him long enough to marry him, but maybe I'm just old-fashioned. I hope they will be as happy as we are."

Good old Brandy. I kissed her. "She will be. This guy Dugan thinks just as fast as she does. Did you hear what he said about Tarsevik? Tarsevik *works* for him, in a way. And here I thought hog-man Bill knocked a lot of apples off the tree when he sold $28,000 worth of hogs."

We went into the kitchen and Brandy fixed a bedtime snack. Shawn was outside in Dugan's car, telling him goodnight. She came in while we were sipping Brandy's special cafe au lait.

"Everything's all set," she said. "We'll be married the fourth of June. Saturday. I counted up and it will be the right time."

"You going after a family right away?" I asked.

"I sure am."

We sat talking about the wedding until I happened to look at the time, and it was ten oclock. "We better get to bed. Have to get up early and be down there ahead of time. I better call down there now."

I called Mom and told her what we had planned to do. When she learned that she wouldn't have to ride up the hill in Tom Larkey's box wagon she was glad, but worried, "If them big wide funny-looking wheels don't jump the track maybe we'll be all right."

Back in the kitchen I said, "Mom's worried now about Aunt Prue going on through again, and about the treads coming off the caterpillars."

"There isn't anything to worry about," Shawn said. "Bill will be on the job." Already she spoke with pride of her man's abilities.

"I can understand how he knocked you off the Christmas Tree in such a short time," I said. "When he wants anything he goes after it like a bitin' sow. I found that out."

Shawn said in a tiny, wondering voice, "He makes me feel like a little kid. I guess it's just love, I guess. No, there's no guess about it. I *know*."

"What did Tarsevik have to say?"

"Not much. He didn't trust me—he's never trusted me. He accused me of staying all night with Bill at a motel last night. We drove to Missouri to get our blood tests yesterday. We stayed all night, all right, but not together...dammit! We stayed at his sister's house. Her name is Mrs. Cartwright—Grace. Her husband owns a drug store, he's got a big wart right on the end of his nose, he's—" and away Shawn chattered, the words gushing like a geyser as they strove to stay even with her rapid-fire mind.

We were ready to troop upstairs to bed when Shawn asked, "Did you give my man the postmark test?"

"Gee whiz! no, I didn't! So many things happened so fast that I forgot all about it. Maybe he took it, at that. Come on!"

We flocked up the stairway and into my den. There it was, in three slotted spaces across the top of a new blank page in the album:

"Love (Kentucky) Shawnee (Ohio) Only (Tennessee)"

14 Saturday morning it was still raining, but it was not the hard, stab-and-splatter rain of the two previous days. We were up early and ready to leave at four oclock. Shawn had resigned her job at the YWCA, to get ready for the wedding, and she was going down to the funeral with Rembrandt and me. On the way to the depot I asked her, "Where did you and Bill meet Simon-Called-Peter Albans on the road?"

She laughed. "Just a little way up from the cemetery. He had his shoes off and was carrying them so he could make better time. What did you call him?"

"His full name is Simon-Called-Peter, according to Uncle LankyFrank. I guess Bill calls him Albans, but Frank calls him Simey. He's Reverend Albans' son, from down in Turtle Holler. Frank said Albans names all his kids after characters in the Bible. He's got another boy named Moses Luke."

"The guy sure could run. Bill ran along behind him at twenty miles an hour and honked his horn, but he splashed to the edge of the road and kept gaining on us. Bill had to go up to twenty-five to catch him."

"Did you pick him up?"

"I just opened the back door and told him to get in and he did. We took him back to the lumber camp."

"What did he have to say?"

"Not a word. He looked too scared to talk. Bill

scared him some more by telling him that he came near being buried, and that probably the next time he found himself in a coffin box he would be."

"You know," Rembrandt said, "when I saw him come out of that box I thought for a moment it actually was Aunt Prue. With that white raincoat and parka he even looked a little like her—thin face, and he was so white. I always thought Aunt Prue looked like a zombie, and as scared as that man was he looked like a zombie or something."

"I'll bet he doesn't drink any more Chinkapin Island whisky for awhile," I said. "He'll probably take up preaching now. His dad wants him to, Uncle Lanky-Frank told me. And if you scare a hillbilly enough he usually turns to God."

"I wonder what Aunt Prue has planned for us today," Brandy said. She still insisted that everything that had happened was not just coincidence, but was brought about by Aunt Prue's witchcraft. "I still feel icky about the funeral."

I was inclined to agree with her, but didn't say so. We stopped at the depot and I checked with Steve Medill to see if the Air Mail Special Delivery Registered letter had come in during the night.

"So you're going to retire, huh?" Steve asked.

"I'm all through. Did that letter show up?"

He shook his head. "Not a thing."

I thought: Aunt Prue is at her shenanigans yet. The letter had had plenty of time to come from Oregon. "O.K.," I said. "Nothing we can do about it now. We'll just have to hold the funeral without it. So long. Thanks for looking for it, anyway. Take it easy. Poke and throw everything right. Work hard and make more money after you get this raise that's pending in Congress so you can kick in more to the retirement fund—work till you're seventy so the government won't have to pay you so long for just breathing."

The Folly had been brought up from the roundhouse earlier than usual, and Aunt Prue was already loaded. I went over to the baggage section to see if the coffin box had been cleated to the drain boards, and it was — with two-by-fours. It was on the right-hand side of the car, the same side the Spunky Ridge hand truck with the milk cans on it would be parked, going south, and right by the door where it would be easy to unload. I kicked at the cleats. They were nailed solidly with spikes. The box wouldn't slide around any this trip, no matter how slick the floor became; nor would it roll if the triple valve acted up. I returned to my car, conscious of having done everything I could to finish off the funeral on this second shot at it.

"The will didn't get here," I told Brandy and Shawn. "We'll have to use Charles' copy."

"Aunt Prue again," Brandy said. "Keep your fingers crossed."

We stopped at Vinton for second breakfast, and having plenty of time, cut through on the old graveled road past the cemetery and on down to Saganois to check on things there. Just before we got to Sny Magrew we met Bill Dugan's cavalcade of caterpillar tractors and bulldozers pulling the long, log-hauling low-boys. His men had erected canvas shelters on the low-boys, which were big enough to haul forty or fifty people apiece. We counted five rigs and a extra cat.

Simon-Called-Peter Albans led the parade with a big yellow D-8 cat. He sat under an enormous white-and-yellow umbrella, but still wore the same wet-weather gear he had worn the day before — white peaked rubber hood and raincoat to match. With his sardonic face, still pale as a zombie's from the overhang of Chinkapin Island whisky, he looked like Mephistopheles on a devilish errand as he came clanking down the road, the D-8 spouting fire and smoke from its exhaust pipe and making a lot of racket.

I risked the rain, rolled the window down, and yelled, "Hello, there, Simey." I had never met him, but I had been highly interested in him ever since he had jumped out of the coffin box the day before. Uncle LankyFrank had told me he was the second best shangler in Spunky Ridge, being topped only by Aunt Prue, who had out-shangled everybody in a contest when she was past 70. And now that she had passed away he was the champion.

I must digress a moment to explain that the Spunky Ridge Shangle is a combination of Cake Walk, Buck & Wing, Turkey Trot, Pigeon Strut, Limber Jim and anything else you can think of that is sinuous and twisting. It's primitive, and like all primitive dances, has overtones of sex.

It originated in the Spunky Ridge hills many years ago when some forlorn hillbilly lover carved an image of himself out of hickory and hinged the joints, even those of fingers and toes. He fastened a control stick to the head and held it in one fist, and with his other fist pounded on a clapboard, keeping time to the cadence of his lament, which might be anything from *Take My Little Shoes Away* to *Barbara Allen*. He sat on one end of the clapboard, on a chair or a stump, with the vibrating end of the board projecting.

By skillful use of the control stick, plus the tempo and varied force of the blows rained on the clapboard, the figure was made to shangle. Sometimes a leg or an arm made a complete revolution. At first these figures were made anywhere up to a yard in height. But later they were made bigger. I once saw one six feet high. It took two men to operate it: One to hold the thing on the board and the other to pound. The next logical step, of course, was to shangle in person.

It was easy for me to picture Simon-Called-Peter Albans as a lovelorn hillbilly sitting on a stump in the woods.

What with all the noise the cats were making, he couldn't hear me when I yelled, but he waved one double-jointed arm and his spooky face grinned.

"He looks icky yet," Shawn said, "but I guess he's sober."

"You mean I have to ride up the hill on one of those things?" Brandy asked.

"Or else walk," I said.

"They're fun, Mom," Shawn gushed. "Maybe I can get you on a cat. I was on one yesterday. I even drove it a foot or so. There's Bill's camp over there." She pointed at an open space in the timber along the Saganois River. "That's the kitchen, and the bunkhouse is over behind it."

We looked and saw Bill's Cadillac parked beside a big gray-and-blue house trailer. "There's my house!" Shawn said excitedly. "The back room is Bill's office. Wait a minute—why don't I get out here and ride back up with Bill?"

I stopped the car. "Do you want to?"

"He's probably asleep. Probably been up all night getting things ready. I'm going over and wake him up. I want to see what he looks like in bed, anyway, before I marry him." Right eye cocked, she got out of the car and in her feminine foul-weather gear went sneaking across the road as though she were stalking a moose.

"I guess she loves him, all right," I said, and felt a tightening in my throat. "The way she's going after him."

"Yes," Brandy whimpered. "She does. She isn't ours any more. I hope it's for the best."

Driving the few miles on down to Saganois we

talked about the possibility of my inheriting Aunt Prue's Cadillac, also perhaps enough money to enable us to take a nice long vacation. Maybe we would even have enough cash to buy us some new clothes, and a new set of false teeth apiece. We both needed new teeth.

At Saganois everything was ready for the second day of the funeral. The Spunky Ridge roads were so bad by this time that Professor Bascom Twog, Aunt Pop Papp and her father and some others who lived far back in the Ridge had stayed overnight in the Saganois Hotel, and were ready to tackle their respective jobs again. The little hotel was jammed. When I drove down to pick up Cousin Bonnie and Charles a NO VACANCY sign was hanging on the knob of the front door.

Only Uncle LankyFrank, of all the far-back Spunky Ridge folks, had braved the mud to go home for the night, and he went back because he had to feed his dogs.

"My Sunny bitch has been ailin' with the pups for two days," Uncle LankyFrank said, "but she was up and hungry at mornglom today. I think ole Sunny will thole through now." He appeared to be far more concerned about his Sunny mother dog than he was about getting Aunt Prue properly planted.

We gathered at Parker's Funeral Home this time to start the funeral procession. Everybody had left the flags on their cars, and it seemed to me there were more cars without flags than there were the day before. By this time, word of the $50,000 insurance policy had spread all over.

By being forced to postpone the ceremonies it looked like Aunt Prue would have a bigger funeral than ever, rain or shine. Her reputation, and remembering her as many people did, caused them to surmise that if they didn't attend the funeral they wouldn't have a ghost of a chance of inheriting any money; while if they were present they might hear their names called. Besides the older, funeral-going people, it being Saturday, quite a few kids who thought it would be fun to ride up Snake Mountain in a low-boy pulled by a cat were going along.

Everyone seemed to be in good spirits, considering all the rain and the fact they were going to a funeral. Cousin Charles still wore his argumentative costume— I noted that he had washed his pants with their built-on feet—and he and Bonnie were still clamoring, but not quite so intensely. Mom was still worrying about the cats sliding out of their treads, but Mom could always find something to worry about.

Even Aunt Millie had found her gestures and her turkey-gobbler's voice. At Parker's she had pumped her arms at me and oogled and googled. I interpreted the sounds she made as, "Did you go to the depot and ever'place and see if the will had come, thataway and that?" I told her I did.

The hearse headed the parade out of Saganois, this time, like any other funeral procession, although of course it still didn't contain Aunt Prue. We left at nine oclock, in plenty of time to meet The Folly at Spunky Ridge flag-stop.

Everything went along just fine. We were waiting in the rain when the little one-car train came rollerskating around the curve just north of the station and squealed to a smooth stop—and I knew the triple valve had been replaced or repaired. Substitute Scott, defying the downpour, hung in the door of the mail compartment in the habitual highbehind slouch: Elbows hooked over the safety bar to keep from falling out, and one foot against the sliding door to hold it from slamming forward and mashing something when Wild Ike Skaderight applied the brakes. Scott saw me and motioned frantically for me to come over.

While the pallbearers were transferring Aunt Prue out of the car, onto the hand truck and then into the hearse, I splashed over to the mail car.

"That letter you were looking for came in on the Zephyr," Scotty said, "from Omaha." He handed it to me, together with a yellow register-receipt card, the standard Form 3830.

"Good boy, Scotty!" I said. "This is what we've been looking for. Looks like things are going to work out a lot better than they did yesterday." I signed for the letter, scrambled back into my car, and showed it to Bonnie and Charles.

Charles touched the brilliant green, built-in binocular pocket of his birdwatching jacket and said, "We can't use the copy I brought down, after all." He seemed crestfallen, and his *Alta Pete* seemed to droop.

The funeral procession, now equipped with a corpse in its hearse, rolled along nicely. It arrived at the foot of Snake Mountain about half past ten. Tom Larkey had installed a new white-oak endgate in his box wagon, and it looked strong enough to keep the heaviest coffin box ever built from sliding through it. However, the wagon wasn't needed; because five of Bill Dugan's yellow cats were lined up, each with a driver under his big two-toned umbrella, and each hooked onto a yellow, canvas-topped low-boy, ready to go up the hill. I apologized to Mr. Larkey for not letting him know we had made a change in arrangements for getting up the hill.

Mr. Parker had decided to have a cat pull the hearse up, and one stood by itself at the head of the line. It was a D-6, smaller than an 8, but still a husky machine. A dozer blade, pulled up as high as it would go, was fastened to its front end. It had a flamboyant umbrella, but no driver.

Simon-Called-Peter Albans ambled over to my car and there was a look of deep concern on his thin face. He pointed back down the road. "Feller got knocked off his cat back yander at that brushy place. Tree limb brushed him off. We're a skinner short!"

"Is he hurt?" I asked.

"Not much, but boss man took him back to Sny Magrew so the doctor could flea him over. Said for me to hook the hearse behind a low-boy and go up thataway, but I ain't got nothin' to hook on with. I guess he'll be back dreckly and drive the 6 up hisself. I guess we better wait for him."

"I have a tow chain in the trunk," I said. "Maybe it'll work."

I was going to give Simey the keys to the trunk, when the black tassel of Charles' yellow fez brushed against my neck as he leaned forward to talk to Albans. "I have had considerable experience with caterpillar tractors. I shall be glad to accommodate you and drive it up myself."

Simon-Called-Peter blinked his eyes as though he had been confronted with a pink elephant. I was too astonished to say a word. The mental picture of Charles in his birdwatching costume on a yellow cat pulling the hearse up Snake Mountain, alta pete, seeking high things, was far beyond anything I could imagine. This could not possibly be anything but Aunt Prue's witchery at work.

Simey's double-jointed eyes wobbled. He gulped two or three times, and when he finally found his voice said, "Back 'er up and I'll hook you on, then. She's already runnin'."

Charles got out in the rain in his bird-watching costume and picked his way daintily through the puddles, trying to keep from soiling his booted white pants any more than he had to. He reached the cat and mounted it.

It was plain that some time in his life Mr. Charles Willard Stabbs had skinned cats. He scrooched the big machine part way around, right and left, a time or two, getting the feel of its levers and pedals, then eased it back to the clevis on the end of the chain that Simon-Called-Peter had fastened to the two hooks on the front end of the hearse.

Simey picked up the clevis, fitted it to the drawbar on the cat, dropped an iron pin through its holes, checked with Mr. Parker's helper, swivel-eyed Latrum Squall, at the wheel of the hearse, and when Latrum lifted a shaky hand to indicate he was ready, motioned for Charles to take it away.

We lined up the low-boys and loaded them with the older folks, but they couldn't haul everybody. Counting kids, there were a couple of hundred who had to walk. Aunt Prue would have loved to see all those people trooping up the hill in the rain and mud, helping themselves along with sticks and dead mullein-weed stalks, ice creepers balling up their feet till they left elephant-size tracks, and trying their best to act like they were attending a funeral. She would have laughed fit to kill.

As though she weren't laughing at that very moment:

I was riding on the rearmost low-boy in the procession. Swinging around the rounces I could see Charles on the leading cat, dragging the hearse. He sat primly under the gay umbrella.

It was unfortunate that Aunt Prue had forgot to request *Yankee Doodle Dandy* be rendered on fife and drum as her funeral cortege negotiated Snake Mountain.

15

The procession swung the last rounce and stopped in front of the iron gate behind which the stone statues of Grandpa and Grandma Dinnegan sat side by side in their concrete armchairs, facing east. Grandpa looked sternly out at his descendants and his bewhiskered face was disapproving. Grandma, however, looked more cheerful, and as though she was enjoying herself. There was a hint of a smile on her face, as though she was about half afraid to laugh out loud when Grandpa was around. She looked a great deal like Aunt Prue.

I have always thought my grandfather Dinnegan looked at me, his Turk-and-Indian grandson, like a bull at a bastard calf. Whenever I had hunted quails on Snake Mountain I never went near his side of the graveyard, and if I killed a bird anywhere near him I sent my pointer dog to retrieve it. No matter at what angle I stood from him he seemed to keep his eyes on me, like an Uncle Sam recruiting poster, except of course he never pointed his finger at me.

Today his stare at me seemed more accusing than ever, I thought, and for good reason – although Jehovah knows I didn't have anything to do with the carnival tent over the grave. The long hard rain had washed all the dirt and grease off of it and both the reading and the picture on its sloping top half stood out in glaring colors: The letters green on white, and a shapely lady in blue tights and a lavender loop of beads with two red spots inside the loop.

IOLA
The Fairy In The Well
Each And Every Part Of Her Entire Anatomy
Quivers Like A Leaf In An Iowa Cyclone
10 Cents

I hurried through the arched gateway and past Grandpa Dinnegan, not daring to glance at Rembrandt or even squeeze her arm, as blushing red as her face was. I wouldn't have been at all surprised if Grandpa had turned his head and yelled at me. Strange things have been seen and heard on ghostly Snake Mountain: A woman without a head, balls of fire chasing people, and on dark and stormy nights something that went "spitza-spitza-spitza."

The mountain had been called Snake ever since years ago a woman who was picking blackberries along Rocky Branch had heard a hiss, looked up and seen a big black hoopsnake rolling down at her. She dodged it just in time and the sticker on the end of its tail stuck in a tree just below her and the tree died before night. The sticker had torn a hole in the hem of the woman's dress as it went past, and the next day when she was patching it she happened to put a ravelin' in her mouth, as a woman will when she patches, and she died right away, still sitting in her rocking chair with her needle and thread in her hand.

Some said that if Bascom Twog had had his madstone there right then he might have saved her life, as it was good for hookworm and chigger bites, but that was long before the Negro preacher had died and given Bascom his madstone. "It was even before Bascom was even borned," Mom told me.

The funeral services had to be held up a few minutes until all the stragglers arrived. By eleven oclock, however, everyone, including Bill Dugan and Shawn, had made it up the hill. I edged through the crowd to where Bill and Shawn stood, out from under the tent, in the rain. The tent wasn't nearly big enough to shelter the huge crowd, and only the first-generation relatives and the dignitaries could stand under it. However, the rain was gradually letting up. It made only a gentle musical patter on the canvas now. "What happened coming up the road this morning?" I asked Bill.

"One of the boys—Rollie Morgan—didn't see a tree hanging out over the road. It knocked him off the cat."

"Hurt him any?"

"Not much—the limb was dead. Didn't even take the umbrella along with it. Morgan'll be all right in a day or two. They were all racing and acting the fool or it wouldn't have happened. Morgan had passed Albans and was two or three hundred yeards ahead, looking back, when the limb knocked him off."

"Who stopped Rollie's cat?"

"Albans. He shut off his cat and ran and caught Morgan's." He grinned. Surreptitiously, I nudged Shawn in her ribs. I've always done that to Shawn under similar circumstances, the more solemn the better, if I think they're funny. I get a kick out of watching her struggle to maintain her dignity and a straight face.

Reverend Alvin Hoosh opened the service. He took his stand on a piece of plywood, brought along for the purpose, in Mr. Parker's artificial grass at the head of the grave, bowed his head, and offered the regular prayer he always opened with, Uncle LankyFrank said, at adult funerals. It was partly his own, but I recognized parts of The Second Epistle of Paul the Apostle to the

Corinthians:

"Father in Heaven, as we gather today to pay our last respects to a loved one... 'for we which live are always delivered unto death for Jesus' sake. Amen.'"

The prayer wasn't long because Reverend Hoosh' asthma bothered him more when he bowed his head. In planning her obsequies Aunt Prue had shrewdly taken into consideration every contributing factor and detail, no matter how insignificant. It was obvious that she had realized she had outlined a long service and wanted it to move right along.

When Reverend Hoosh finished praying he lifted his head, opened his Bible and read several passages from the same source that he had taken his opening prayer:

"'For we know that if our earthly house of this tabernacle were dissolved, we have a building of God, an house not made with hands, eternal in the heavens.'

"'While we look not for the things which are seen, but at the things which are not seen; for the things which are seen are temporal; but the things which are not seen are eternal.'

"'Knowing that he which raised up the Lord Jesus shall raise up us also by Jesus, and shall present us with you.'"

He was barely able to finish the last verse. His ailment made speaking difficult, and the longer he talked the more he wheezed. I felt sorry for the old fellow. Aunt Prue should have been spanked, asking him as she did to conduct her funeral.

We couldn't see his long-horn mustache while he was praying, but when he raised up his head to read from his Bible it began to flutter. It moved noticeably, no matter what word he spoke, even if there were no breeze at all, but on words with b, f, p, t, or v in them not even a zephyr was required to make it quiver.

Double ss's activated it, too, and ph's and th's. There wasn't any breeze at all today, but at that Shawn didn't dare meet my eyes.

She and Bill stood outside the tent, but Rembrandt and I rated cover. So did Professor Bascom Twog, because of his zither. He stood beside me, with Bonnie and Charles behind us. The five of us were down toward the foot of the grave, with Reverend Hoosh and his daughter Aunt Pop Papp at the other end. Ranged down along each side of the casket, which of course had been taken out of the coffin box by Mr. Parker and Latrum Squall, were Mom and Uncle LankyFrank and the other close relatives.

Mr. Parker had brought along one folding funeral chair, forgetting, I suppose that there would be two preachers, and Mr. Hoosh and Aunt Pop alternated at sitting in it. They kept popping up and down, off and on, thataway and that, all through the service.

When Reverend Hoosh finished reading the introduction to the sermon he sat down and Aunt Pop stood up on the piece of plywood. She was a huge woman, with a thin high-bridged nose, commanding in appearance, dressed in black. She possessed a great shelf of a bosom and was proud of her possession. The only other bosom I ever saw that was as big as Aunt Pop's was on a Wisconsin bar maid. She used hers to carry two glasses of beer at a time to customers. With a beer in each hand, she hauled four glasses, and she made a fortune.

Cousin Bonnie had finally finished the obit, and Aunt Pop was ready to read it. Her pulpit-trained voice ended all sentences on the standard high dangling note:

"Miss Prudence Dinnegan was born April 1, 1874. She was the daughter of Hugh Dinnegan and his wife Cornelia Dinnegan, nee Sprunge. In the War Between the States her father played a drum.

"Mrs. Persnosky attended school at first at Shake-Rag schoolhouse in Starbuck County, Illinois, in which county she was also born. It was three miles from the school to her home. She traveled widely, all over the world. A willing woman, nevertheless, if given the opportunity she was glad to struggle."

Aunt Pop didn't have a chance to read the obit ahead of time because Bonnie had finished it only that morning and hadn't handed it to her until we had all gathered under the tent. It was obvious that she wasn't completely familiar with Bonnie's literary style. A puzzling hesitancy was apparent in her delivery, and there were times when she forgot to end her sentences on her high professional note:

"Mrs. Persnosky married Mr. Phineas Persnosky on 16 March 1895 on a packet boat, which was tied up for the winter at a spot on the Ohio River near Cincinnati, Ohio. No offspring resulted from the marriage, which was the deceased's greatest diappointment, and one that she struggled mightily to prevent."

I kept watching Mom as all these sad things about Aunt Prue were being read. Mom had her extra handkerchiefs and her bottle of camphor in her big pocketbook if anybody broke down and took it hard. Her quick black eyes darted here and there through the crowd, but nobody was crying, let alone wailing. Some looked as though they were trying hard to be polite and not laugh.

Mrs. Papp realized she was sounding ridiculous. She began to ad lib, transpose, reconstruct and otherwise edit the obit; and she got to going so fast that she forgot all about the rules of elocution, enunciation and the diction of good delivery and started to live up to the nickname Professor Twog had bestowed on her.

Cousin Bonnie and Charles were standing right behind Rembrandt and me, at the very edge of the tent.

I felt a tap on my shoulder and eased around as unobtrusively as I could so as not to distract Aunt Pop. Charles, although he had lost out on his offer to Cousin Bonnie to trade the wearing of his raincoat over his bird-watching costume for the elimination of her *Lost Moments conte*, had put on the coat in deference to the circumstances, and thus some of his glaring colors were covered. However, he still wore his yellow fez. Its black tassel tickled my neck as he leaned forward and whispered, "If you think this is badly written wait till you hear *Lost Moments*." His aristocratic butler's face crimped with pain.

I shook my head in sympathy and glanced at Bonnie. Her face was radiant, and the blue dimples that were her eyes set deep in her puffy face sparkled with pride. Bonnie at last was having her literary work presented to the public. This day was the greatest in her life.

The obit was originally five typed sides long, but with Aunt Pop's editing and as fast as she was chattering it lasted only about a side and a half:

"The deceased was well-educated attending no less than six colleges and universities in Canada this country Asia Africa Europe and Australia three of which she was graduated from Casner in Cashwellington, Iowa in 1922 Brannigan of Linehan, Illinois in 1928 Bancroft Business College (pop) Excelsior, Illinois (popping nose) in 1933 she also studied at musical lavatories(pop-pop) laboratores she was apt to be driving across the land past a college and admired the trees around it and would stop (pop-pop-pop) enroll and graduate from it she spent many years traveling with amusement concerns (pop-pop) doing missionary work in foreign countries and sold ice cream in Baghdad (pop) and did trapeze work in Australia and India also (pop) magic she leaves to mourn her passing pop to the Great Beyond one brother Frank Dinnegan and three sisters Mrs. Molly pop Padoley Mrs. Maud pop-pop Dinnegan Dooks Miss Millie Dinnegan all of Saganois Illinois (pop) Starbuck Cunty and scores of relatives of a lesser degree interment was in well-known Dinnegan cemetery atop Snake Mountain upon the arrival of the casket from Oregon except one day."

Aunt Pop, utterly pooped, sat down in the chair that Reverend Hoosh had just risen from. It was plain to see that she was disappointed at her recent performance, She put the obit in her habit, the black expansive left-side bulge of it, and from her right-hand bosom drew forth another manuscript. I saw her jaw set in determination. She was going to at least glance at *Lost Moments* before she started to *give* it.

Reverend Hoosh, now standing on the speaker's plywood board, announced:

"'I am the resurrection, and the life; he that believeth in me, though he were dead, yet shall he live: And whosoever liveth and believeth in me shall never die.'"

In spite of all the restrictions Aunt Prue had placed on holding an ordinary beautiful and dignified funeral service for her, Reverend Hoosh and Mrs. Papp did very well.

When Reverend Hoosh found himself running short of breath he stepped back toward the chair, but Aunt Pop was still sitting in it. She had nodded at Susie Spoon and May Hicks, the two girls who had been engaged to sing at the funeral. Now they stepped forward with their song books. They were both beautiful girls, with the beauty of youth if with nothing else.

With no music to guide them, they made two false starts, and then they sang a hymn I had never heard before, something about not having to cross Jordan alone. Their voices although high and thin, had a degree of harmony.

By this time the rain had stopped altogether and the sun was shining brightly. The soaked earth welcomed its warmth and became alive. Hungry birds, forced by the rain to stay sheltered for so long, appeared as though by magic. They chirped lively accompaniment to the hymn about not having to cross Jordan alone as they searched diligently for food. A red fox squirrel flirted his busy tail as he scampered along the top of the iron fence around the cemetery.

As I stood reverently listening to the song and wondering if May and Susie would sing all the verses or only the first and last one, Bascom Twog nudged me and whispered, "I wonder if they will want *Turkey In The Straw* right after this."

"I don't think so. They will preach the main sermon next." It was slow talking, the way we had to be so careful not to be noticed by anybody.

"What will I sit on when I play?"

"Sit on?"

"I need something to sit on so I can hold it on my knees. You have to play a zither flat."

"Gosh, I don't know," I whispered. "There's only the one chair and we don't want to take that. One of them has to stand up all the time now."

16 In the minute or two that I had to think about providing Bascom with something to sit on before the song ended. I caught myself wishing the Jordan song had more verses, to give me more time to think. It wouldn't be safe to forego the zither playing, now that we had followed Aunt Prue's instructions to the letter, so far.

May and Susie finished the hymn, Aunt Pop stood up in preparation of the next phase of the service, and still I hadn't solved the problem. I was frantic.

"Four score and eight years ago," Aunt Pop elocuted, "There was born to Mr. and Mrs. Hugh Dinnegan, of Spunky Ridge, Starbuck County, Illinois, a daughter, their first child. She was the first manifestation of their profound love for each other; a ray of sunshine in their young lives."

I had thought sure Aunt Pop was going to announce the zither solo when she stood up, and I breathed easier when she didn't. With her first words I knew she had launched her allegorical sermon about a bright sun about to set. By this time it was high noon and the sun was shining straight down, but I don't believe anyone was aware of the inconsistency, especially those who were outside the tent watching the wiggles of Iola, the Fairy in the Well, in the little breeze that had come up.

It was along about half past nine in Aunt Pop's allegorical obsequy that I felt the tickle of Charles' *Alta Pete* tassel on my neck again as he leaned over my shoulder and whispered in my ear:

"I have my bird-watcher's seat with me if you want to use it."

I jumped. Mrs. Papp was really a good speaker. I had become so interested in listening to her that I had forgotten momentarily about the matter of a chair for Mr. Twog.

"You mean you got it with you?"

His tern face crinkled in an affirmative as he kept a steady eye on Aunt Pop.

"Where is it?" I whispered.

With Aunt Pop talking as she was, we couldn't say much or move much for fear of distracting her. Charles drew back his raincoat. "Here. Feel."

I had never seen a bird-watcher's chair, or even heard of one, but it was logical to assume that there might be occasions when, watching certain birds, a seat would be extremely convenient.

"It telescopes," Charles whispered in explanation.

Bascom Twog, who had also felt the chair, edged closer to Charles. "May I use it?"

"Certainly."

"Let's see that thing," I breathed.

Rembrandt, standing next to me, noticed the commotion we were making. She edged her regal head slowly around. "Shh," she whispered. "Be quiet."

Working as quietly as he could, Charles unzipped a slit in his pants leg and pulled out his chair. Untelescoped, it looked like a pogo stick with a hinged fork on one end. Folded between the two prongs of the fork was a corded fabric four or five inches wide, something like a saddle cinch.

Charles whispered, "It is adjustable to the height and weight of the user, as well as to the conditions underfoot." He edged forward beside me, and sawed-off Bascom got behind us and fitted the chair to his bottom, his knees so they were level, and the rain-soaked ground. He rose and nodded a triumphant O.K. at us.

I looked gratefully at my cousin-in-law or whatever relation he was to me. I had never liked him any too well but I was in the process of changing my mind. On two occasions today, once with the cat and now with the seat, he had solved problems; had come through with colors flying. The problems had been minor ones, it was true, but they had existed nevertheless. Charles had proved to be a blessing in the disguise of a bird-watcher.

I was elated. I felt we were finally winning the struggle to hold Aunt Prue's funeral and do it the way she wished it to be done. The obstacles she had confounded us with seemed to be growing less and less formidable, and we were overcoming them immediately.

When Bascom finished adjusting the bird-watcher's seat it was noon by Aunt Pop's sermon. The minister was still bearing down on Aunt Prue's religious zeal.

As the minister advanced steadily toward supper-time, I fitted the meaning of her words to my own life. It was four or five oclock in the afternoon of my day right now. Soon it would be dark. If I were going to enjoy myself before my bedtime should come it was high time I was doing it. Because once in bed and asleep I would wake no more.

Aunt Prue's funeral service wasn't maudlinly sentimental, but was significant, therefore more impressive. The people listening to the sermon didn't look like they were attending a funeral. They didn't shift their weight restlessly from one foot to the other, wishing it would end. Instead, they stood enthralled and entertained, examining their own lives. Several times

I noticed signs of merriment on lips that were forced to purse to keep fun from popping out. For Aunt Prue's witchery included even the preparation of her own funeral sermon! She had moulded her life to fit the sermon instead of Aunt Pop doing it the other way around. And she had written Aunt Pop's standard, stockpile, sundown eulogy herself. Thirty years ago!

Aunt Prue didn't hate people, she loved every one of her fellowmen. In Abou's angel's book of gold her name was certain to appear. Rembrandt had merely misinterpreted Aunt Prue's fun-loving spirit.

I didn't realize quite all of this until several week after her death, when I was going through the huge collection of postmarks she willed me. She had four big albums filled with them, besides a lot of loose ones. Across the top of the first page of her No. 4 album was:

"Prue (Oklahoma) Speaks (Texas) Herlong (California) Peculiar (Missouri) Monument (Colorado, Kansas, New Mexico, Oregon, Pennsylvania)"

17

Mrs. Papp had reached the nightglom of the allegorical sermon, and was talking about Aunt Prue's earthly house that had been dissolved, and the other house that she was entering into: The house of the spirit, unable to be seen:

"For this ye know, ye who have The Great Faith," the minister finished, "the house that is not seen is eternal in the heavens. Grace be to you and from the Lord Jesus Christ."

She sat down on the chair that Reverend Hoosh had just vacated. Pastor Hoosh stepped forward, extended his arms, and bowed his head in prayer:

"'...who comforteth us in all our tribulation, that we may be able to comfort them, which are in trouble, by the comfort wherewith we ourselves are comforted by God.' Amen."

Mrs. Papp changed places with her father again and nodded at Susie Spoon and May Hicks. The two girls stepped forward and raised their voices in *Shall We Gather At The River?*" Down at the bottom of the far slope of Snake Mountain we could hear Rocky Branch roaring bank full. Overgorged with the long hard rain, it piled along, thundering over its enormous rocks. Its distant muted elegy was a roll call question: *Shall We Gather At The River?*"

There were many others besides myself who were aware that Rocky Branch was at that moment flowing by "the throne of God." When the hymn ended, Mrs. Papp looked levelly out at us and said grimly:

"Mrs. Persnosky was a great lover of the arts, particularly literature and music. She requested that a sample of each — which she selected herself — be made a part of her last rites."

The pain in the minister's voice was unmistakable. There was a pained expression on her face, too. I had watched her when she first glanced at what I assumed correctly was the script of *Lost Moments*. She had gasped almost audibly.

"She took an intense interest in the writing career of her niece, Mrs. Bonnie Dooks Stabbs," Aunt Pop said, "and has requested that one of the products of Mrs. Stabbs' pen be given at this time."

Again the black tassel of Charles' yellow fez tickled my neck. "One," he groaned in a whisper. "She never wrote but one." His face and whisper contained more grief than I had yet seen or heard demonstrated during the entire funeral service.

"The title is *Lost Moments*, by Bonnie Dooks Stabbs."

Aunt Pop drew a long shuddering breath and plunged in:

"Hello, Stupid," Jack Jackson said, as he shut the door.

"Hello, Balmy," June Johnson said, as she led the way to the living room.

"Well, Toots, what will we do tonight? Go to a tavern or to a dance or to a show?" Jack Jackson then asked.

"Oh, Balmy," June Johnson said hysterically, "can't we merely spend one night at home and look part of the time at television?"

This was something I found difficult to forgive Aunt Prue for torturing us with. Of the collection of college degrees she had, at least two were in English.

"No," Jack Jackson said, very mad. "You always want to stay home and watch some silly television program," he then said desperately.

"Jack Jackson, what's the matter with you? Every time you come over any more you quarrel and act mad. Henry Hendrickson never acts like you do," June Johnson said in a casual tone.

"Who cares about Henry Hendrickson! You think I don't know about your being an artist and having Henry Hendrickson for your teacher?" he said sneeringly.

I looked at Rembrandt. At funerals her face is always composed, her expression dignified. I felt the extreme need for both composure and dignity, and thought that by looking at my wife I would acquire some of hers immediately. Brandy's face, however, was beet red.

Then I looked at Bonnie. Her moon face was jubilant. She looked as though Heaven had just opened its gates to her. I was awed.

"Jack Jackson was a tall man with black wavy hair

and ebony eyes, with snappy features and a smile that would win anybody. June Johnson cared for him as a friend only, but Jack was in love with June.

"Jack Jackson, you can't say things as that," June said with her hands on her hips and looking at him through her blonde curls.

"O, can't I?" he said and pushed at her.

I was forced to admire Aunt Pop Papp's oratorical skill and gallant fortitude. *Lost Moments* was taxing her elocutionary abilities to the utmost but she was staying with it and more than holding her own. Her timing was perfect and she squeezed from Bonnie's *conte* every bit of nuance the piece contained. I began to feel poetic as I listened to her meet each new challenge fair and square by just *a-givin'* it her flair.

Aunt Pop finished *giving Lost Moments* in a resounding and dramatic finale that left us all overflowing with emotion. So moving had been her delivery of the tender love story that in the entire group of grievers there was hardly a dry eye.

Cousin Bonnie's face reflected the glory of her *conte*. I was glad that she had fixed the scratched part — Jack Jackson's unexplained intoxication — that had puzzled me. All her life she had been working on this *conte* of hers, and now that it had at last been smoked out, thanks to Aunt Prue, she was overwhelmed with ecstasy. She broke right down and took it hard; and Mom hurried to her with handkerchiefs and camphor.

Mrs. Papp required several moments to gain control of her own emotions. When she did, she stooped to whisper something in Reverend Hoosh's ear. Mr. Hoosh nodded. Evidently they were a little uncertain as to the best place in the ceremony to insert *Turkey In The Straw* on the zither.

Finally Aunt Pop faced us resolutely. There was resignation in her voice as she said:

"As I mentioned before, Mrs. Persnosky was quite fond of music. She asked to have the well-known folklore classic, which you will presently hear rendered, as part of her funeral rites."

Mrs. Papp as much as told us that while *Lost Moments* was bad, *Turkey In The Straw* was worse, especially when it was rendered on a zither; and that she wanted nothing whatever to do with it. Here's the way I thought she felt: She was familiar with weeping of all sorts at the funerals she conducted, but not when the tears came from laughing. That was what made her feel and act the way she did.

She nodded at Bascom, made her father get up off the chair, sat down herself and stayed there until after everything was overwith, reading of the will and all.

I felt so sorry for Aunt Pop that I whispered to Bascom, "Hold it down a little; don't go after it so ramtujinous." He said he would.

He had already adjusted the bird-watcher's chair and now he eased himself down into its webbed seat and laid his zither across his knees. His hands moved around over the instrument like sorcerer's wands. His fingers, now and then, here and there, thataway and that, plucked a string or two, as he edged gradually into the lilting tune. Then he increased the tempo until he was shuffling along nicely, but not stomping.

I was well satisfied with the way the funeral had gone — so far. And Aunt Prue surely couldn't throw any more monkey wrenches in the works now. Once *Turkey In The Straw* was ended, Mr. Parker and shaky-handed Latrum Squall could open the casket, we could file past and take a last look at our relative, and that would be all except the reading of the will, after the grave had been filled.

I wondered how many times it would be necessary to go through *Turkey* in order to satisfy Aunt Prue —

and decided three would be enough. I knew Bascom would become so absorbed in his music that he might not want to stop for quite a long time, as he had done at the Left Hand Hill Store, but I could always go over and kick the pogo-stick chair out from under him and stop him that way.

The tune was going along smoothly, and inside their boots and overshoes everyone was tapping their toes in time to it. *Turkey In The Straw* is a lilting piece of music that gets down into a hillbilly's blood and stirs it until it craves action. I felt as though I could make the loose ends of floor boards in a new hayloft clatter a little myself, old as I am.

Then, all at once, Aunt Millie, who had stood like a statue all through the funeral, began pumping her arms and gobbling:

"Oogle google, goo-goo, google-oogle goo; google-oogle, google-oogle, google-oogle goo."

I could never make out Aunt Millie's gobbler's jargon, except a word now and then, even when she wasn't grieving; and now that she had broken down and was taking it hard I couldn't understand what she was trying to say at all. Mom's prediction had come true; Aunt Millie had broken down at last. Oh, but she went on!

"Oogle google, goo-goo, google-oogle goo; google-oogle, google-oogle, google-oogle goo."

Mom hurried over to Aunt Millie with her camphor and handkerchiefs but was afraid to get close to her, the way Aunt Millie was swinging and pumping her arms, thataway and that. Mom tried to quiet her from a distance by saying, "Now, now, Millie, don't you cry and go on. Remember the Lord giveth and the Lord taketh away, and they ain't nothin' fairer than that."

Aunt Millie paid no heed to Mom. She had cleared a little space all around her and was carrying on bad. Uncle Parley Dooks and Aunt Maud were listening closely to what Aunt Millie was trying to say. Aunt Millie made her home with them and they could understand her better than anyone else could.

I was about to go over and chouce my hysterical aunt and try to calm her down, when I thought I detected a faint rhythm in her gobbling. It might be my imagination, but I didn't think so. I listened closely. If I wasn't mistaken, Aunt Millie's googles had the same tempo as an old-time square-dance chant:

"Sheep and a hawg a-walkin' in the pasture,
"Sheep says,'Hawg, can't ye walk a little faster?'"

As though in answer to the request for more speed, Bascom Twog stepped *Turkey In The Straw* up until he was very near stomping, in spite of what I had told him. And Aunt Millie was keeping right along with him:

"Bob-cat and Tom-cat a-walkin' on a rail,
"Bob-cat a-steppin' on the Tom-cat's tail."

I made my way around the edge of the tent to where Aunt Maud and Uncle Parley were standing close to Aunt Millie. Just as I cam up to them, Aunt Maud grinned a big wide smile, bigger than any I ever saw on her face in my whole life. She was sort of weaving first one way and then the other, in time to the music — and so was shuffling old Uncle Parley.

I nodded toward Aunt Millie, and said to Aunt Maud:

"She's taking it pretty hard, maybe I better chouce her and hold her arms and try to make her stop crying."

"She ain't cryin'," Aunt Maud said. "She's *callin'*."

That's what Aunt Millie was doing, sure enough:

"Chase that rabbit and chase that squirrel,
"Chase that pretty girl arowwwnd the worl'."

The only way I could think of to make Aunt Millie stop taking it hard was to have Bascom stop the music. I motioned at him but he didn't see me, bent over his zither as he was. I started back toward him. I would kick the bird-watcher's seat out from under him if I couldn't stop him any other way.

By this time Bascom was thoroughly warmed up, and was not only stomping, but galloping. He was going like a man in a hurry, picking fly-specks out of pepper; he was the Devil beatin' tan-bark; he was going after that old zither like a bitin' sow.

In spite of all my efforts, the funeral had gotten completely out of my control. There was no more dignity to it than there was to a hog-scald. Everybody except Al Hoosh and Aunt Pop were at least smiling, and many were snickering out loud. The breeze had freshened, and I could imagine how Iola, the Fairy in the Well, was quivering.

I was desperate. I tell you, it was a weary, trying to think of something to do that would bring the funeral service back to where it should be. Aunt Prue wasn't in the well yet. The way things were going was downright sacrilegious.

I hadn't quite reached Bascom when Aunt Prue's witchery suddenly came to my rescue. The bird-watcher's chair, what with Mr. Twog's considerable weight swaying it first one way and then the other as he tapped his foot and kept time, all at once sunk into the mud clear up to its fork. Bascom fell back on his caboose with both feet in the air. *Turkey In The Straw* gave one last twanging squawk, as though somebody had grabbed it by the neck and was wringing it.

Even the two ministers guffawed. So did everyone else—except me. I stepped out in front of the sprawled Bascom and raised my arms.

"Please!" I yelled. "Behave yourselves! This is a funeral! Save your monkeyshines till later!"

18

My words didn't have the authoritative, rebuking effect on the crowd that Aunt Maud's "Shut up!" always had on Uncle Parley, but they served their purpose. There was considerable tittering still going on amongst the young people on the outer edge of the crowd, who were in a better position to watch Iola do her show, but they really couldn't be blamed for being amused. The breeze was rising steadily, and had loosened the tent stakes that had been driven into the mud, and the looser the canvas became the more varied was Iola's performance.

Bascom Twog scrambled to his feet, brushed at the mud on the seat of his pants, and deplored in a whisper to me, "Plague on such hyjelogical weather! Ground so soft it would mire a jacksnipe!" To Bascom, all weather was either hyjelogical or hijelogical. It was hijelogical, now that the sun was shining brightly, but the last two days it had been hyjelogical. He telescoped the birdwatcher's seat back together, handed it to Charles, who put it back in his pants.

With Bascom back on his feet, and Aunt Millie's arms quieted, we were ready to take up the funeral service where we left off. There wasn't much left to do except lower the vault into the grave, wait till Lafe and Wally Barnes, assisted by Latrum Squall, filled in the dirt, and then read the will.

Reverend Hoosh stood at the head of the grave as Mr. Parker raised the lid of the casket. As we filed past Aunt Prue for our final look at her there was much suppressed emotion but little that overflowed. For Aunt Prue wore such a happy little grin that even Mom found it difficult to shed a tear.

There were 486 people at Aunt Prue's funeral. I know the figure is correct because, the way things turned out, it became my job to know; not only how many mourners were there, but also who they were.

Not all of them filed past the casket but there were quite a few. It was a good half hour before all those who wished to view the remains had done so. Nobody went home, however, they just waited around to learn what was in the will.

Finally Mr. Parker stepped forward and closed the lid of the casket and that of the vault. The nearer relatives moved back under the tent and arranged themselves as they were at first. Reverend Hoosh stood ready to deliver his final short prayer. Mrs. Papp still sat in her chair.

I held my breath, kept my fingers crossed. I still had the uneasy feeling that something outlandish would happen, even then. Something would explode, Uncle Parley would shuffle too close to the open grave and fall in, a meteor would fall close enough to Charles to splatter mud on his still-immaculate white-rubber pants, or some other ridiculous incident would transpire.

Nothing happened. The vault settled gently. The interring equipment was removed. Lafe and Wally Barnes shoveled the first dirt into the grave. Latrum Squall, from the outside edge of the pile of dirt, helped them.

Reverend Hoosh bowed his head and murmured, "May God keep you and be with you always, sister

Persnosky." Even with all the esses delivered in the freshening breeze his long-handled mustache didn't swoosh.

I never felt so relieved since I don't know when. Aunt Prue was in her grave now and was being covered with dirt. There certainly wasn't anything to feel swizzly about now.

How wrong I was! More than once, in the immediate future, I was to recall Aunt Prue's mischievous grin as she lay in her coffin. She might have passed away in the flesh, but her vexatious spirit was still going as strong as ever.

While the Barnes boys were filling the grave and rounding it up I hunted Charles and drew him off to one side. "Charles," I said, "I still feel squeasy about this funeral. Can you think of anything we didn't do right?"

"No, I cannot," he said in his precise voice. "However, I too am apprehensive—perhaps because of the unseemly entertainment provided by the lady on the tent."

The carnival tent that had once sheltered The Fairy In The Well had high sides, obviously designed to cover a platform reached by a short flight of steps. Customers probably leaned over a railing and looked down on Iola, who performed in a mirror-lined box.

I looked up at Iola, who was doing her stuff on all four sides of the tent, and saw what Charles meant. The rippling breeze was causing the buxom girl to quiver like a leaf in an Iowa cyclone, all right, as advertised, and every once in a while the ten cents looked like a dollar. Iola's rear rippled like those of televised football players set to guard their goal, and an airplane flies over. Moreover, the sun now shining so warmly, was gradually contracting the soaked guy ropes, thus providing the dancer with an astonishingly varied repertoire.

"Maybe we should strike the tent," I said, trying to imitate Charles' flawless delivery of words.

"I believe it would be merciful," he said.

I caught Mr. Parker's attention, and by a series of gestures got across to him that it would be a merciful thing to do to strike the tent, and he said something to Latrum Squall and Lafe and Wally Barnes, so that the upshot was we all were standing in the open in the sunshine when it came time to read the will.

Cousin Bonnie had been fooling around the statues of Grandpa and Grandma Dinnegan, and now she came waddling over to us and interrupted, "What are you two doing here all by yourselves, just talking?"

I knew what she craved. "That was a nice piece of writing you did on the obit, Bonnie. It would have been better if Aunt Pop hadn't got excited and talked so fast."

"Thank you," Bonnie beamed. "How did you like my *Lost Moments*?"

"That was interesting. I can understand why it was one of Aunt Prue's favorite pieces of literature."

I could also understand why Bonnie's literary agent coined such phrases as "divine afflatus" and applied them to her. A few hundred hopeful, perennial beginning writers like Bonnie — at a reading fee of a dollar a thousand words — on a literary agent's list of clients would provide him a nice annuity, though he might become a bit fed up in time with June Johnson, Jack Jackson and Henry Hendrickson.

"I'm going to write it as a television show," Bonnie said, "and after that I'm going to novelize it again. I novelized it once, and I can use the same protagonists and secondaries, but I shall have to create some new tertiaries."

"I think so too," I said.

As Bonnie waddled away, Charles said, "That was nice of you, Boley."

"Rembrandt has a weakness, too: Got flowers all over the house, even in my den. Sometimes I have to set the dam' things down off the windowsill onto the floor before I can see out."

"Bonnie's lieterary ambition outweighs her creative ability," Charles said. "However, her hallucination provides her with considerable pleasure, is harmless and economical — and brings a good book into the house occasionally. I probably never would have read *Caine Mutiny* or *By Love Possessed* if Bonnie hadn't been a would-be writer."

"That's like me. If it wasn't for Rembrandt's flowers I never would have learned the difference between a lilac and one of those stinky tuberoses. But what I wanted to talk to you about is this swizzly feeling about the funeral. Do you think it's anything connected with the will?"

"That is all it could be. That is all there is left."

"Do you suppose I should read your copy instead of mine?"

"That is ridiculous. What possible difference could that make? One copy is the same as the other."

"Look, Charles, Bonnie told me about the will when she first got here. She told me she was going to get most of Aunt Prue's money — except a dollar apiece to a few of the others. Is that true?"

Charles looked at me steadily. "I cannot tell you."

"You know, don't you? Weren't you present when she made it out? Didn't you help her?"

"I helped her."

"I just want you to know that it doesn't make any difference to me, one way or another, if I don't get even a dollar. Money doesn't mean as much to me as it does to most people. I don't need much money in order to be satisfied—just enough to buy a book now and then, and some ammunition for my guns."

"You go ahead and read your copy of the will. That will be in compliance with Aunt Prue's explicit instructions. Do not, however, be surprised at the nature of its contents."

"You could tell me now, what to expect. I'm going to be nervous enough, as it is, when I get up there."

"You can read your copy now and obtain the identical information. Why don't you?"

I reached down in my pocket and drew out the letter from Oregon. I had put it in the big shell pocket of my duck-hunting parka and buttoned the flap so I wouldn't lose it. It was a heavy brown Manila envelope, important looking with all its postmarks, stamps and registration number.

"I don't want to open it here. I want to open it up there at the grave, where everyone can see me do it."

The cold fact of the matter was that I was a little afraid to go up there so near Aunt Prue and open her will and read it. If Charles would give me a hint of the nature of the thing perhaps the shock would be lessened considerably. Something might even pop out of the envelope and bite me or something.

"See here, Charles, I never knew you very well before this funeral. I guess we've become better acquainted the last few days, what with everything we've gone through, than we have in all the years we've known each other. IF you know what's in the will, tell me. Might save me from fouling up like Aunt Pop did with the obit."

"No, Boley," Charles said sympathetically. "I'm just as anxious about it as you are, and I understand how you feel. So I'm certain you understand why I refuse to divulge the contents of the last will and testament I helped Aunt Prue prepare several years ago. However, I shall be glad to supply you with certain information obtained from the research and statistical departments of my company, regarding people in the Octogenarian Plus category, which may prove helpful. This category, I might add, is becoming more and more important to insurance companies, due to the steadily increasing longevity of the American people. Hence the desirability of comprehensive study in that field. Within the framework of the research program, for example, there is considerable work being done in geriatrics, with which more and more Americans are vitally concerned."

Charles wore a yellow fez with a black dangling tassel. He had on a jacket of hunting-shirt red, with a patch pocket of glaring green. His gleaming rain-washed white pants had feet in them. He stood practically at military attention, his raincoat draped neatly over one arm, now that it had stopped raining. I was awed.

"Our research department is almost ready to publish a comprehensive report concluding that when people attain Aunt Prue's age they lose much of their normal sensitivity and clarity of thought. Particularly do they react differently toward tragedy—even death—from what they did when younger. Perhaps it is because they have lived out one phase of life—the physical—and are subconsciously longing to lead a different one, of the spirit. Certainly there is a psychological factor involved."

Utterly fascinated, I watched Charles' thin lips as they formed words and delivered them in pear-shaped tones:

"Such changes might be induced by a hardening of the arteries, resulting in retarded circulation, and affecting adversely the normal functioning of the intellect. They become puerile in many aspects of their thinking. Children, we know, accept death as a matter of course, and as long as they remain children are far more practical about it than adults are. Aunt Prue might have developed a syndrome that had attained its apogee when she prepared her will."

"I think so too."

Just then Gib Parker stepped away from the graveside and motioned at us, so I was saved from the embarrassment that comes from ignorance. Charles and I found our wives and made our way over to the gathering throng of hopeful grievers. Aunt Prue's grave was rounded up neatly and covered with flowers.

I pushed the hood of my parka farther back so to be sure I was bareheaded and stepped up on the pulpit board. Rembrandt stood on one side of me and Bonnie on the other. Charles was next to Bonnie, and Mom and the rest of the close relatives flanked us right and left.

I looked out at the crowd. Their expressions were subdued and reverent. At last they looked like people who had come to a funeral.

I reached down dramatically and withdrew the envelope from the shell pocket of my parka. When I opened it there was a second envelope, sealed with red gum. The crowd gasped audibly at the delayed climax. I broke the seal.

Glancing at Bonnie, I noticed her eyes were wide with expectancy and hunger. I looked at Charles. His face was knowing with a possum-eatin'-poultry expression.

The will had been typed on a single sheet of legal-looking paper. As I unfolded it my fingers shook; and I could sense the hushed expectancy of the mourners.

In my years of distributing letters in a bouncing, swaying mail car I have mastered the trick of reading a complete address in one quick glance, and can tell whether or not there is anything unusual about it. This acquired skill, however, was wasted on the will.

I took one look at the document—and guffawed! I couldn't help it. I couldn't have kept from laughing if I had known it would kill me. Everyone else at the funeral had laughed at something or other—except me, who had been too concerned with keeping things moving along to laugh. Now it was my turn. I laughed fit to kill.

I handed the will to Bonnie. "Here, cousin," I choked, "you read it."

No wonder Aunt Prue looked so mischievous in her coffin. For extending cattycornered across the entire length of the page, in what looked to me like Cherries-In-The-Snow lipstick, was Aunt Prue's unmistakable scrawl:

"THIS IS NO GOOD!"

The signature was complete, followed by her habitual, clinching, piquant "Pee-Pee."

19 All the way back to Saganois I kept breaking out in the belly-shaking sniggers. I tried to keep from doing it but just couldn't. That monkey-silly will was the most hilarious and ridiculous piece of buffoonery I ever had anything to do with. "Why in the devil didn't she just tear the dam' thing up if it wasn't any good?" I howled. "What did she want to keep it around for?"

Rembrandt was ashamed of me. "Stop your nonsense," she said, "or else let me drive. You'll run us in the ditch."

Mom, in the back seat with Cousin Bonnie and Charles, appreciated the humor in Aunt Prue's chicanery. "She sure tricked us," Mom said, "thataway and that. I figured she was a-coddin' us when I looked at her in her coffin. I've seen that grin on her before."

The Stabbs didn't consider the incident funny. In fact, Bonnie looked as though she was about to bawl; and Charles' polite smile, when he managed one, was forced and sheepish. He said, "I presume she made a more recent testament."

"I presume she did, too," I said, "but I have presumed so many things about Aunt Prue that never turned into anything but presumptions that I'm tired of presuming. I presume she's dead, too, but it wouldn't surprise me a bit if she was waiting for us in Saganois when we get ther—with her broomstick parked in in front of the house. That silly will beats the b-Jesus out of me!"

"What shall we do now?" Bonnie asked plaintively.

When I regained control of myself I said, "I don't know —have everybody meet at Mom's and hold another conference, I guess. That's what we've been doing every day. We don't want to miss today."

"Had you read the will when you handed it to Bonnie?" Charles asked in a cross-questioning voice.

"No, I only read the lipstick part."

"The will may be declared valid," he said ominously.

His bobber was down, I knew. He was resorting to his knowledge of legal matters, a field where he knew I would vanish into the first plowed furrow, merely in order to inflate his ego back to its normal pressure.

"Maybe it will," I said, "but that's something for the Probate Court to decide."

"Would you like to read the will now! I have a copy, you know. He hesitated, then said pointedly, "No more than half an hour ago you begged me to divulge its contents to you."

"Go ahead."

"'Chicago, Illinois,'" Charles read in his expository voice. "'July 3, 1953. I, Prudence Persnosky, being of full legal age and of sound and disposing mind and memory and not acting under duress, menace, fraud, or undue influence of any person whomsoever, do make, publish and declare this my *last* will and testament and I do hereby expressly revoke any and all other and former wills and codicils to wills heretofore made by me.'"

"Do you have to read the whole thing?" I cut in. "Can't you cut out some of the flub-dubs?"

"A will is a vital, legal and dignified document," Charles said stiffly. "It should be perused and presented with meticulous attention to details."

"Sort of *given,* huh?"

Rembrandt kicked my shin, and I let Charles finish reading the ponderously worded deposition without again interrupting him. Scattered amongst the whomsoevers, wherefores, hereinafters and hypothecates was what I guessed was the reason for Cousin Bonnie's look of despair and Charles' deep chagrin:

Bonnie was willed $10,000, sure enough, but it was to be used to "promote her literary career." I figured the promotion stipulation was the sticker that was stinging the Stabbs.

Uncle LankyFrank, Mom and her sisters came in for equal shares, but all the lesser relatives were remembered with only a dollar apiece. I drove on, thinking of my dollar wrapped up in that absurd lip-sticked will. I could see that comical, silly-fool scrawl yet: THIS IS NO GOOD, Pee-Pee! I exploded.

At Mom's house, her next-door neighbor, Mrs. Plink, had dinner ready when we arrived. Mrs. Plink had been ailing for some time and had felt so poorly that she couldn't go to the funeral, so she stayed at Mom's and got dinner. Said she might as well, thataway and that. She was nearly as old as Mom, small and shriveled, and as spry as a flea.

We all trooped in the house and went to work on the ham and chicken and other grub that was piled on the huge boarding-house table in the living room. Everybody talked at once, trying to decide what would be the best and most logical thing to do next.

Professor Bascom Twog suggested that we write to the lawyer Mr. Stambo and inform him as to what all happened. "I suggest that somebody besides Mrs. Dooks do it, however," Bascom said.

Aunt Pop Papp looked at Mr. Twog warmly. "I am afraid Mrs. Dook's literary ambitions will never be fulfilled—in fiction. Perhaps she should try articles or photo-journalism. Why don't you do it, Mr. Paydoley?"

"Shucks," I said, "I couldn't write down everything that happened any more than I could fly with the geese. I might call him up after dinner, though. Let's see, what time is it out there? Would he be in his office — this is Saturday?"

I had dropped Cousin Bonnie and Charles off at the hotel so Charles could get out of his bird-watching gear. Cousin Manford was going to pick up his sister and her husband and bring them out to Mom's for dinner as soon as Charles changed clothes. They were late getting there but we didn't wait on them to eat. We were hungry by this time, as it was half past one oclock and the most important Spunky Ridge meal of the day should have been eaten an hour ago.

When Charles came in the house I saw his eyes find Belshazzar, Mom's saucy cockatoo, and fix the bird with a long studious stare. The parrot could say a few words that had been taught him by railroad men and highbehinds, for instance, "Casey Jones," and "Ball the jack," and "High wind and heavy traffic;" also every time the phone or the doorbell rang, or he heard anyone step up on the porch, he blared out, "Katerr, katerr, somebodyatthedoor, somebodyatthedoor, Jesus Christ, somebodyatthedoor, katerr, katerr!" He seemed to fascinate Charles.

After everyone had eaten dinner we found our respective conference seats in Mom's big front room. We had held so many conferences on Aunt Prue's funeral by now that we subconsciously reserved our seats, as people do when they eat at the same table hand-running: Aunt Millie, Aunt Maud and Uncle Parley on the couch; Cousin Manford, Uncle LankyFrank and I on the davenport; Edith Dooks, Aunt Birdella and Rembrandt on a love seat; Mom in her telephone chair with the arm-rest and tablet and pencil; and the others, including Bill Dugan and Shawn, scattered around on the floor or wherever. Only Cousin Bonnie and Charles, dignitaries of the family who were attending the conferences for the first time, had to seek new seats. Bonnie sat at the dinner table where she could nibble surreptitiously, and Charles carted a kitchen chair over where he could keep a watchful *Alta Pete* eye on Belshazzar.

We were going after our problem like chattering magpies when the telephone rang a great long jingle. We all guessed it was a long-distance call. Mom jumped up from her telephone chair and hurried to put Belshazzar's cage hood on him, to make him shut up, for he was squawking at the top of his chirp that somebody was at the door Jesus Christ!

I sat down in Mom's chair, lifted the receiver and said hello.

"Mr. Paydoley? John Stambo again. Efficient group of operators you have in Saganois, they found you right away. How was the funeral?"

"All right. We just finished it. Had to postpone it a day. Had a little bad luck and some rainy weather.

"Did you open the will and read it?"

"Yes. Well, no. I guess it was cancelled. I was just fixin' to call you about it."

"We found a later will this morning when we searched her car. It was the the glove box. She made it out down in Las Vegas, Nevada two months ago."

Las Vegas, I thought. So Aunt Prue had been having fun right up to the last. Probably she had pulled some of her old packet-boat and Klondike gambling tricks down there. She had probably cleaned the place out. "That explains why she marked the one you sent me 'no good.'"

"She appointed you executor. You couldn't come out

here for a few weeks, right away, could you? The Court convenes the twenty-fifth—that's a week from Monday—April two five."

"Gosh, I don't believe I can go away out there. Don't think I can get away that long, anyway. Don't have much vacation time accumulated."

I had forgotten that I was retired; that I didn't have to get up at four oclock in the morning any more unless I wanted to hunt or fish; that I had $764.36 in the bank; that Rembrandt had mentioned taking a long vacation.

"All your aunt's property must be sold," Mr. Stambo continued, "even her car and her scintillometer. The real estate in Florida, too. It will take a little time, and considerable correspondence, before all the conditions of the will are met. You may even have to go to Florida."

"Florida! Gee whiz!"

Bill Dugan got up off the floor and came across to me, bent down and whispered, "Go ahead." He took the pencil that was lying on the arm of the telephone chair and wrote on the pad there, "Stay long ncssry. You-Rem need vacatn. Take Cad. I use yr car."

I looked up at my future son-in-law. It had taken him only about two minutes to make arrangements with my hillbilly relatives to build a road up Snake Mountain. As Mom put it, he was *in*.

"All right," I told Mr. Stambo. "I'll be there."

I hung the receiver up and for a few seconds nobody said a word. Then Charles nodded at the bird cage and asked Mom:

"May I remove his cover now?"

20 Rembrandt and I left Windfall the following Monday morning in Bill Dugan's new Cadillac. The car didn't do such a mundane thing as run, it drifted, effortlessly, silently, heavenly. I certainly wouldn't want to drive it with its speedometer out of commission. I found myself doing sixty-five miles an hour lot of times before I realized I was making such speed, and would slow down.

Out across Iowa we went the first day. Farm tractors spluttered forth and back across the acres of rich black soil that would in the next few months produce millions of bushels of grain—and in spite of government-suggested reduced acreages set new production records.

The second day we crossed Nebraska, with all its whitefaced Hereford cattle grazing tails to the prairie wind, turning end for end only to splatter; and rolled into Wyoming with its mountains and its oil derricks and refineries showing up regularly along Route 30.

The third day we dropped down through a rocky canyon to Salt Lake City, and drove a hundred miles across the salt flats into Nevada, and I thought about the story about the motorist who stopped at an isolated gas station to tank up. He asked the station man, "You don't happen to know where John Smith lives, do you? This is his address but I don't see any houses."

"He lives here," the station man said. "Down that side road there. It's just about a hundred miles down to John's place. First house on the left."

Toward Reno the fourth day, and ate lunch at Harold's Place, where gambling went on twenty-four hours a day seven days a week, and played all the rackets, losing only two dollars; and then we climbed famed Donner Pass into great golden California. "California, here we come," we sang.

Rembrandt and I were on the first vacation we had taken together since 1932, when the Dirty Thirties depression raged, from which no postal employe has recovered financially to the extent required to afford a prolonged vacation, especially if he is bringing up a family. We were having the time of our old lives, here at five oclock in the afternoon of them.

"I never seen such a country," I kept saying.

"The word is saw." Brandy would patiently correct me.

"Saw might be correct back in Illinois," I'd say, "but it ain't a big enough word for out here. I never seen such a country." We acted like a couple of kids.

The Cadillac drifted into Pistol River, Oregon the afternoon of the fifth day. The town sat on the bank of the Pistol River, which emptied into the Pacific ocean. I caught several fish in both the river and the ocean while I was there.

Mr. John Stambo was a nice friendly chap, about what I had expected him to be from talking to him on the phone. He had been a buck colonel in the Air Corps during World War II. I had been in the Air Transport Command, so we had some good war stories to tell each other. I also became acquainted with the boys around the court house; I met Mr. Charley Wang, the undertaker; and the man who ran the motel where Aunt Prue died, and who spelled his name Tczetl, pronounced Tootle. Mr. Tootle took me fishing one afternoon while Brandy and Mrs. Tootle shopped.

Aunt Prue's verified Last Will & Testament went through the legal processes like thin soup through a horn, as we say down in my old home country of Spunky Ridge. It had been prepared with such skill and care that not a single loophole was in it. Its stipulations were the same as those in its predecessor – the one that Aunt Prue lipsticked – with the exception of the disposal of a fifth of the insurance money.

I had guessed correctly about the promotion of Bonnie's literary career being the sticker. In her last will, Aunt Prue had left Bonnie the ten grand only if she could show, as proof of her writing ability and good faith, at least one acceptance by a publisher of books or by a magazine of national circulation of something she had written. This my cousin could not do.

Aunt Prue knew that Bonnie would have to work her divine afflatus overtime if she was ever going to write anything worthwhile. She waited a long time – until after Bonnie had brought up her family and thus had more time to work and study – before she changed her will and left the money to The Mountain Home Orphanage, at Cincinnati, Ohio. It was a golden opportunity for would-be writer Bonnie Dooks Stabbs but she was unable to grasp it.

There was a typical Aunt Prue trick apparent even in her last will. She left Bonnie her battered old portable typewriter; and to me she bequeathed her huge collection of postmarks, which came from all over the world, but mostly from the Middle East, where she had lived several years. She was a much better writer than Bonnie; she even composed little stories – *contes*, I guess they were – and all unprintable. One about three brothers explaining to their father how they escaped from an extremely amorous situation even shocked me. Its last line was "Calcutta, Baghdad and Timbuctoo!"

I accepted my lone dollar in the spirit in which I knew it was given: that of fun. Out west silver dollars are much in use, so I got one and had a jeweler mount it for me on a tiny silver tripod. It makes an excellent paperweight.

Every person who had attended the funeral was willed ten dollars, merely as a favor. It was quite a job to find them all, or learn their addresses. But with the help of Mom's griever's book and her astonishing memory I was finally able to mail checks to all.

Aunt Prue's Cadillac was sold, and so was her scintillometer. Out in that wealthy, uranium-fevered section both sales were easy to make. The disposal of the Florida real estate was a little more difficult. Rembrandt and I were obliged to go down there, so we returned to Illinois via Florida, a not unpleasant obligation.

We visited son Fred and his family in San Francisco, but left before boredom set in, wandered leisurely down the coast, then went in and out of Mexico before heading east. As we rolled along—took us three days to cross Texas—we tried to decide where in great grand America we would prefer to be when darkness settled, if we had any choice in the matter. The miles of open country where a hunter could fire a 30-06 without risking killing somebody appealed to me, but Brandy preferred the gentler existence along the Gulf coast.

"But it won't get dark for awhile, kid, I hope. I've got to make some gunstocks first."

"Going to have an electric-light bill of a thousand dollars a month, after all, Boley?"

"Funny how things turned out, right from the start, when Stambo called at four oclock that morning: Running into a son-in-law, and retiring and everything.

By the way, do you still think Aunt Prue was a witch?"

"I don't know. It's difficult to believe that all the absurd things that happened were coincidental, but I suppose they were. People can't project their personalities or their spirits after they are dead. Several have tried to – Houdini did – but nobody has ever done it for sure."

"For sure – that's the important part. Nobody is sure whether it can be done or not. Smarter people than we are have tried to settle the question and they're no farther along than when they started."

"If Aunt Prue was a witch she was a lovable one. And I was right about her loving children and wanting some of her own – I'm glad the orphanage got the money."

"It may be," I said, "that, knowing Aunt Prue to be the kind of person she was, as everyone concerned with her funeral did, we subconsciously expected her to act the fool, even at her own funeral. Maybe we brought all those silly stunts on ourselves without realizing it."

"But you were obligated to follow her instructions."

"Not necessarily."

Brandy was astonished." You wouldn't dare not to!"

"And there you are! All I know is Aunt Prue was grand old American gal. She started out young and helped develop this country to where it is today. As Aunt Pop said in her sermon. 'She had The Great Faith!"

We finished our business in Florida and headed north. Dilapidated, broken-backed shanties where Negroes lived in Georgia and the Carolinas sported television antennas, and electric washing machines on their front porches; stone fences bordered the highways of Virginia; Washington, D.C. was inspiring – every American should visit it. Brandy and I spent a week with son Roman and his family in an apartment a hundred feet up an elevator shaft, but we didn't like it much in New York City. For inlanders like us there was too much touch-and-go, too much glitter, too many people with tragic faces.

New England was a little more to our liking. The rock-dotted hills reminded me of Spunky Ridge, although they were much better groomed. In them was an explanation of the Boston accent, as well as an indescribable sense of solidity.

We drove the turnpike back to Chicago, and stayed a week in our favorite metropolis, where we started housekeeping in one room and alcove with bath on the third floor of an old mansion at Forty-fifth and Grand Boulevard many years ago. We parked near Soldier's Field, almost on the exact spot where the plane carrying the first mail into Chicago landed in May of 1919. The airport was a patch of weeds then, with two red drums of gasoline, and the wavering tracks of a truck that had hauled thehm from the city out to Grant Park. The plane brought two pouches of token mail from New York—one containing Iowa letters and circulars, the other South Dakota. In the Union Station mail terminal at the corner of Jackson and Canal streets I distributed the Iowa to fast-mail connections, while a fellow clerk worked South Dakota.

Brandy and I arrived back at Windfall a week before Shawn's wedding. There were so many things that had to be done around our house that it was an entire day before I found time to examine all the postmarks Aunt Prue had left me. They had been shipped in a big box. Some were in albums but many were loose or had never been cut from their envelopes.

It was when I looked at the last numbered album that I saw Prue Speaks Herlong Service. I wrote to Mrs. Carrie Papp and asked her if she had written her allegorical sermon herself, or did Aunt Prue write it? The minister replied that my aunt had composed the first draft, but that it had been revised several times by her.

"It happened so long ago — in 1925," Aunt Pop wrote, "that I don't remember exactly which part Mrs. Persnosky wrote and which I wrote. I do know that Mrs. Persnosky's life inspired me to make any changes in it that I might have made. She had The Great Faith."

Aunt Prue had The Great Faith, sure enough: in God, in her country, in the spirit of fun. The only evidence I have of her ever entertaining a serious thought I found on the back of an old envelope in among the loose postmarks she left me. She had scribbled:

MY SPUNKY RIDGE
Prongs and pinnacles, rivers and hills;
Green — then brown — the bewhiskered hills;
Yellow-clay banks where the groundhog drills.
Rocks and ridges and eroded banks;
Brush and thickets and wild-grape hanks;
Existence earned by laborious yanks.
Mountains and gullies and steeps that rounce;
Slopes down which the walnuts bounce;
Hunt in the high weeds — foxes jounce!
Rocks and trees and birds and air;
Grassy glades and flowers fair;
Sun and stars — and God — are there.
               So may be I.

--30--

www.ingramcontent.com/pod-product-compliance
Lightning Source LLC
LaVergne TN
LVHW041615070426
835507LV00008B/254